Wonderful Rooms
Where Children
Can Bloom!

—— ● ——

Other Books by Jean R. Feldman

Kids' Atlanta

A Survival Guide for Preschool Teachers

*The Complete Handbook of Indoor Games
and Activities for Young Children*

Transition Time

Science Surprises!

Wonderful Rooms Where Children Can Bloom!

Over 500 Innovative Ideas and Activities for Your Child-Centered Classroom

by Jean R. Feldman

Crystal Springs
SDE BOOKS

a division of Staff Development for Educators
Peterborough, New Hampshire

© 1997 by Jean R. Feldman

Printed in the United States of America

13 12 11 10   6 7 8 9

Published and distributed by:

Crystal Springs Books
Ten Sharon Road, Box 500
Peterborough NH 03458-0500
1-800-321-0401

Cataloging-in-Publication Data

Feldman, Jean R. 1947-
         Wonderful rooms where children can bloom! / by Jean R. Feldman.—1st ed.
[224]p. : cm.
Summary : This title shows how to create a warm, inviting room where children in
K-2 classrooms can learn and explore. Includes hundreds of creative activities and
learning center ideas.
ISBN: 978-1-884548-14-7
1. Classroom learning centers. 2. Teaching. 3. Learning. 4. Early childhood
education—Activity programs. I. Title.
372.21—dc20   1997   CIP
LC Card Number: 97-67533

Publishing Manager: Lorraine Walker
Editor: Aldene Fredenburg
Cover, Book Design, and Illustrations: S. Dunholter
Production Coordinator: Christine Landry

This book is dedicated to

Frances Bethel,
my friend and department chair
for many years. Thanks for
encouraging me and giving me
a job where I could grow!

Acknowledgments

"Soup from a stone, fancy that!" Remember how everyone contributed to make the wonderful soup in the folk tale, *Stone Soup*? So it is with *Wonderful Rooms,* where so many teachers have shared their creative ideas for helping children grow.

To all of you I say, "Thank you!" And the teachers who use this book as a resource, and the children whose lives are touched in a small way because of those ideas, will say, "Thank you," too!

Contents

Share the Wonder!

Surround children in beauty.

Embrace them with love each day.

Share their wonder of discovery.

Share their joy as they play.

Help children be successful.

Make them feel special, too.

With choices and hands-on learning,

They'll grow and learn as they do!

Give children peace and happy memories.

Create warm and inviting rooms.

Cherish all of the children.

And they will surely bloom!

There is a powerful relationship between environment and behavior. If we want children to feel comfortable, confident, secure, and happy, then we must create beautiful schools where they can grow and develop to their fullest potential. In a world where children spend more waking hours in school than they do in their own homes, the need to provide them with warm, nurturing spaces is particularly important.

This book shows you how to create these nurturing environments, in your school and in your classroom. *Part One* gives you ways of making your whole school an inviting place for your children and their parents, inside and out. *Part Two* takes you inside your classroom, giving you many ideas on making your physical space attractive. This section also deals with such practical matters as portfolios and teacher storage tips.

Part Three tells you how to create a literate enviornment; *Part Four* shows you ways to use your children's art as a main focus in planning your room.

Learning centers are invaluable in creating a child-centered environment. *Part Five* is devoted entirely to learning centers, providing management and documentation tips as well as lots of ideas for creative, fun activities in a number of different centers.

Young children learn by playing; *Part Six* gives you many games that will challenge your children's minds and build their skills while letting them have fun.

Wonderful Rooms Where Children Can Bloom! is meant to be a resource for creating a meaningful and dynamic classroom where all children can grow in their own unique ways. These ideas can easily be adapted to reflect the personalities of your children, community, and program. It is a challenge and it is work, but children are worthy of the most beautiful, happy, loving, and exciting schools we can give them!

In, Out, and About

Ideas for Enhancing the Ambiance of Your School

Little things count—little children, and all the little things you do in your school to create an effective learning environment. This chapter will offer you ideas for:

- landscaping and road appeal
- inviting lobbies
- a parent resource center
- playground fun

Out Front— Road Appeal

How your school looks from the road reflects your philosophy and what's happening inside. Check these out:

- Drive past your school. What kind of first impression would it give to others?

- Is there an attractive sign with your school's name?

- What is the landscaping like? Are the bushes trimmed? Is the curb manicured and free of debris? Is the grass well-maintained?

- Are the driveway and sidewalks clean and in good repair?

- Is the building well cared for?

Try these ideas!

- Let the children plant flower beds in the front of the school, or use decorative pots of flowers by the front door.

- Use seasonal displays, such as pumpkins, scarecrows, a flag, or wreaths.

- Put a "welcome" mat by the front door.

Lovely Lobbies

The lobby gives a first and lasting impression of your school. These ideas will create a warm ambiance.

Senses:

How does your lobby smell when you enter the school? Fresh flowers, plants, baking bread, or potpourri can add pleasant odors.

Do you hear the happy sounds of children? Children's musicians or the voices of children in your school singing on a tape are more positive than commercial radio stations.

Is the entrance sunny and well-lit? Window treatments, a comfortable seating arrangement, pillows, and children's art will create a positive, home-like environment. Rather than hanging adult art and posters, use pictures, murals, and three-dimensional projects created by the children in your school.

News:

Use an easel or dry erase board in the lobby to remind parents of schedule changes, special events, and other news.

Input:

A suggestion box will let parents know you value their ideas.

Album:

Keep a photo album in your lobby with up-to-date pictures of all the activities in your school. Also, capture field trips, parties, and other special moments. Children and parents will enjoy recalling memories as they look at the album. (It's also fun to make a video of the children and play it in the lobby for parents.)

Family Tree: ∙∙∙∙∙∙∙∙∙∙∙∙∙∙∙∙∙∙∙∙∙∙∙∙∙∙∙∙∙∙∙∙∙∙∙∙

Ask each family to bring in a family photograph. Glue the photos to construction paper cut in geometric or seasonal shapes (leaves in the fall, flowers in the spring, etc.). Punch a hole in the ornaments and tie them onto a plant or artificial tree with ribbons.

VIP Family: ∙∙∙∙∙∙∙∙∙∙∙∙∙∙∙∙∙∙∙∙∙∙∙∙∙∙∙∙∙∙∙∙∙∙∙∙

Choose a family each week to highlight, and make a poster to display in the lobby. Include pictures of family members and pets, and information on employment, hobbies, favorite foods, etc.

The Parent's Place

The role of parenting can be supported by a resource library in your school.

Materials:

- parenting books (ages and stages, discipline, sibling rivalry, etc.)
- pertinent articles on parenting (bedtime, ADHD, single parenting, health issues, etc.)
- audio- and videotapes on parenting topics
- bookshelf, table
- comfortable chairs

Directions:

Place the books and videos on a shelf in your lobby. Articles can be organized by topic and stored in a file box. Have parents sign out materials.

Variations:

Encourage parents to add to the resource center by sharing books or articles that have been helpful to them.

Create an eyecatcher for children in the lobby, too. It might be an aquarium, a school mascot (a large stuffed animal), a Big Book display, an antique school desk, or a box sculpture designed by children.

Outdoor Fun

Care and planning should also be devoted to the outdoor play area. Besides having fun, children develop important social, language, motor, and emotional skills as they play outside.

Enchanted Garden

Materials:

- garden spot
- child-sized garden plants
- seeds or bedding plants
- large rocks
- waterproof paints, old brushes

Directions:

Involve the children in preparing the soil by letting them dig in the dirt several days prior to planting the garden. Let them decide what flowers they would like to plant, and guide them in planting the seeds. Help children find large rocks and paint them, then outline the garden with the rocks. Encourage the children to take responsibility for watering the garden, pulling the weeds, etc.

Variations:

Use tubs, planters, or old tires for a garden.

Plant vegetable seeds that the children can harvest and eat. Call it your "soup garden."

Plant flowers in colorful rows to resemble a rainbow, or plant red, white, and blue flowers in the shape of a flag.

Music in the Air

Materials:

- bells, wind chimes
- ribbon or string

Directions:

Tie old bells or wind chimes to the branches of a tree with ribbon or string. When the wind blows, the tree will sing to you.

Fitness Trail

Materials:

- poster board
- markers
- clear contact paper
- string

Directions:

Involve the children in creating a fitness trail for the playground. It might include doing jumping jacks, going down the slide, climbing a pole, riding a tricycle, etc. Let them number the activities, write the directions, and draw pictures on the poster board. Cover with clear contact paper, then use string to tie at different points on the playground.

Fence City

Materials:

- wooden fence
- outdoor paints
- brushes

Directions:

Let children design a city they would like to paint on the fence. After drawing it on the fence with chalk, let the children paint it.

Variations:

On wooden fences, paint animals, trees, trains, or other objects that children can incorporate into their dramatic play.

Sidewalk Fun

Materials:

- sidewalk paint
- old brushes

Directions:

Design different objects and games that you can paint on your sidewalk. You might do four squares, hopscotch, geometric shapes, silly footprints to follow, road signs, etc.

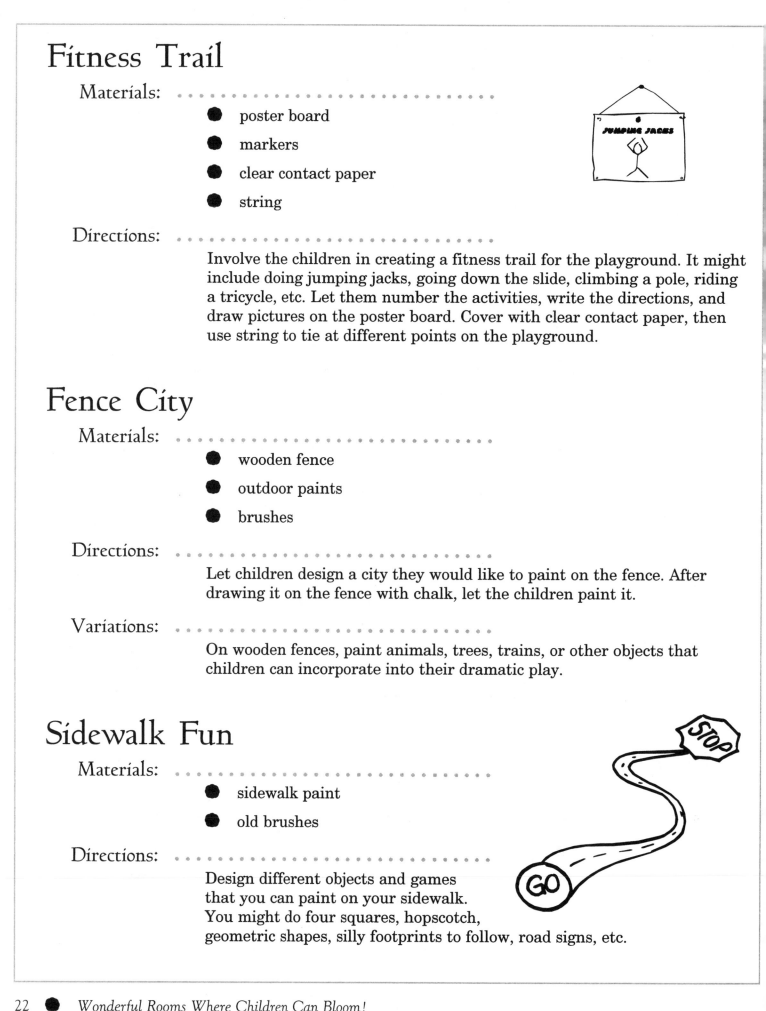

Roll-a-Rama

Materials: . . . .

- clear plastic pipes (4'-10')
- duct tape
- small cars, balls, or toys

Directions: . . . .

Tape the pipe to the fence at an angle. Children can put the toys in the top end and watch them roll out the bottom.

Variations: . . . .

Have children put toys into cardboard tubes so they can watch them roll out the other end. Use different-sized tubes from wrapping paper, laminating film, carpet, and fabric.

Purchase plastic drain pipes at a hardware store and use in a similar manner.

Windsocks and Pinwheels

Materials: . . . .

- windsocks, pinwheels, banners, and flags

Directions: . . . .

Attach windsocks, pinwheels, flags, pennants and banners to fences and trees on the playground.

Variations: . . . .

Let the children make the flags and pennants with old sheets and markers.

Nature Center

Materials: . . . .

- bird feeders
- animal cage
- rocks, trees, bushes, and natural items

Directions: . . . .

Create your own nature center with feeders, animals, a rock garden, etc.

Talkie Talkie

Materials:

- 2 plastic funnels
- 6'–8' clear tubing (size the tubing to fit into the ends of the funnels)
- duct tape

Directions:

Tape the funnels to the ends of the tubing. Put one funnel at the top of a playground climber. Use duct tape to secure the tubing to a post so the other funnel is about two feet from the ground. Children can talk back and forth to each other through the funnels.

Fence Painting

Materials:

- sheet of Plexiglass
- drill, wire
- tempera paints, brushes

Directions:

Drill holes in the top of the Plexiglass and attach it to the fence with wire. Let the children paint on the Plexiglass, then just hose it down to clean it.

Variations:

Hang a shower caddie on the fence to hold paints.

Let children fingerpaint with shaving cream on low windows or a Plexiglass easel.

Give children old ribbon or plastic strips to weave through chain-link fences.

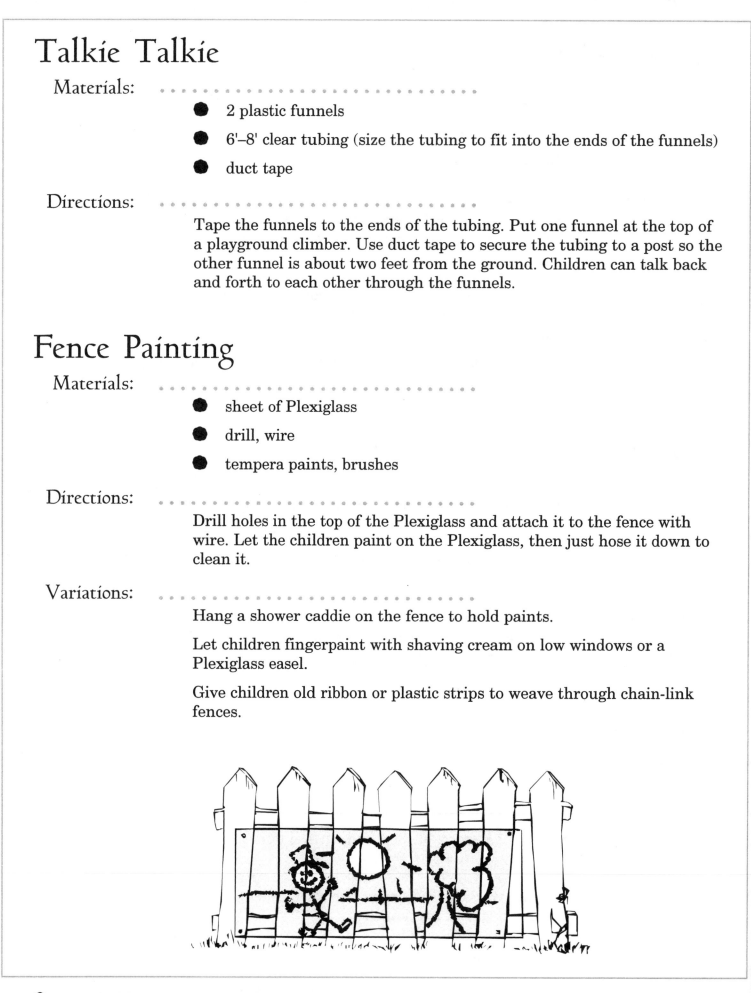

Mailbox

Materials:

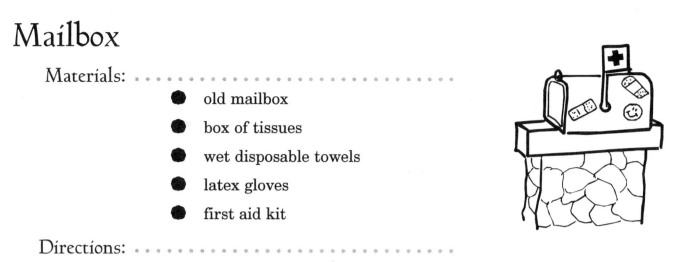

- old mailbox
- box of tissues
- wet disposable towels
- latex gloves
- first aid kit

Directions:

Mount an old mailbox on the playground and store first aid supplies and tissues in it for emergency situations.

Creating Your Wonderful Room

Consider these three A's in designing environments for children:

Aesthetics is the love of beautiful things. Clearly, for children to learn to appreciate beautiful things, they must be surrounded by the best we can give them. According to research studies, children are happier, get along better, concentrate better, and have a more positive attitude about themselves and school when they are in a beautiful environment. The aesthetics in your school can be enhanced by following these guidelines:

Focus—Children, their activities, and their art should be the focus of the room. They should provide the color.

Light—Make the classroom as light as possible, with large, open windows. Pull up blinds and shades to capitalize on natural lighting.

Neutrals—Keep the walls light and use neutral colors. Use wooden furniture, shelves and equipment when possible.

Softness—Add pillows, soft sculpture, rugs, and window treatments to make the room look like home rather than an institution.

Nature—Bring the outside in with plants, pets, flowers, rocks, shells, and other natural objects.

Senses—A variety of textures, sounds, sights, and smells should surround children. Fresh air, flowers, evergreens, shaving cream for fingerpainting, and the aroma of food cooking will add a pleasant odor.

Order—Provide children with a sense of order and avoid clutter. Group like objects together and organize the classroom so children can take out materials and put them away independently.

Balance and Harmony—Too many toys, posters, and objects in the room create visual overload and interfere with children's learning. Make the classroom interesting but peaceful, with a balance of pictures and materials. Rotate toys and games to maintain children's interest.

Detail—Pay attention to little details. Take the time to carefully arrange and display children's art.

Ambiance refers to the mood, character, and atmosphere in the school. Children should be immersed in harmony, warmth, and acceptance when they walk through the door. Everything about the school, from the furniture to the artwork, should say, "This is a place for children. This is a place where children come first." These principles can have a positive effect on creating the ambiance you desire in your school:

Ownership—Create a truly child-centered classroom by including children in decisions about how to set up the classroom and decorate areas. Ask them which areas they like or dislike and why. How would they make the classroom better? What would they do if they were the teacher?

Size—Furniture, sinks, door handles, and other fixtures should fit the size of the children. Adapt equipment and spaces for children with special needs.

Eye Level—Display the children's art and materials at their eye level—not at the adult level.

Privacy—Create cozy spaces and distinct areas where children can play in small groups. (Children are more likely to run around with large, open areas.)

Sound—Don't overwhelm children with noise. Keep your voice down and the children will model you. Use classical music or other peaceful music to quiet children.

Safety and Security—Clean, safe environments will help keep children healthy and will make them feel secure.

Attitude suggests respect for individual children and their families. Children should be encouraged to make choices, laugh, play, and learn in their own unique ways. The classroom should be set up like a children's discovery museum, with many open-ended activities. Attitude about children and how they learn is reflected in the following:

DAP—Use developmentally appropriate practices and materials to enable children to explore, be independent, and feel successful.

Play—Play is what children do best and enjoy most. It is their work, and should be integrated into all areas of the curriculum.

Friends—Encourage children to interact with their friends by talking, questioning, and helping each other. Use cooperative groups to work on projects.

Meaning—Provide children with authentic learning experiences that grow out of their interests and issues important to them.

Activity—Children learn by *doing!* They need to move, use their senses, talk, and interact with concrete materials.

Modeling—Modeling is one of the most powerful ways children learn. Demonstrate what you want children to do, and they will imitate you.

Repetition—Allow children to repeat activities and experience a wide variety of materials, so that skills are reinforced.

Success—It's true: nothing succeeds like success! Create an environment that is risk-free, where all children can feel worthy and competent.

Diversity—reflect the diversity of all the people in our society with bias-free pictures, toys, books, and materials that represent different sexes, ages, abilities, and cultures. Celebrate how people are alike and how they are different!

Wholeness—Learning should be connected and integrated into all areas of the curriculum. Education should also be focused on the *whole* child by meeting his or her physical, social, emotional, and intellectual needs.

Look Up! Look Down! Look All Around!

Add variety and interest to the classroom with these ideas.

Look Up!

Materials:

- scarves, strips of fabric

Directions:

Loop the scarves or fabric under ceiling tile beams to create softness and diffuse light.

Variations:

Hang a kite, windsock, or birdhouse from the ceiling.

Tape pictures to the ceiling so children have something to look at when they nap.

Let the children decorate the ceiling tiles with paints or markers. They might illustrate alphabet letters, numerals, their families, friends, etc. (Be sure to get permission from your principal before doing this!)

Look Down!

Materials:

- colorful pictures of pets, people, food
- clear contact paper

Directions:

Put the pictures on the floor and cover them with clear contact paper.

Variations:

Put children's photographs or artwork on the floor and cover them with the contact paper.

Use colored tape on the floor to make lines, shapes, or letters on which the children can walk.

Attach footprints to the floor to show children where to line up.

Look All Around!

Materials:

- colored cellophane, Saran Wrap, or acetate tape

Directions:

Tape sheets of transparent colors to windows at the children's eye level so they can look through them out the window. (Tape just the top edge so children can lift the colored sheets.)

Variations:

Let children paint windows with tempera or other washable paint.

Make portholes through which the children can look. Cover the bottom portion of the window with black paper, then cut out circles and other shapes.

Back It Up

The backs of exposed shelves can provide another learning area for children.

Materials:

- felt and flannel board story pieces
- chalkboard
- wipe-off board
- glue

Directions:

Cover the back of a shelf with felt.

Mount a wipe-off board to the backs of furniture.

Attach a chalkboard to a wall or shelf. (Add a small basket with chalk and an eraser.)

Use mirrors on the backs of equipment.

Variations:

Display children's art or photographs on the backs of shelves.

Tape large sheets of paper on the backs of shelves, then let children decorate with crayons and markers.

Invisible Walls and Wall Hangings

Here are some unique ideas to break down large areas and create cozy spaces. These hangings can also be used on walls to add softness and texture.

Handprint Sheets *

Materials:

- old sheets (white works best)
- paint
- pie pans

Directions:

Pour the paint into the pie pans. Let the children dip their hands in the paint, then apply them on the sheet. Hang from the ceiling as a divider.

Variations:

Children can also decorate sheets with fabric crayons or markers. Older children could sew buttons, ribbons, lace, or felt shapes on old sheets to make wall hangings.

Fabric and Scarves *

Materials:

- strips of bright-colored fabric or scarves

Directions:

Hang fabric or scarves from the ceiling to add softness and to separate areas.

* To hang, insert jumbo paper clips in the top of the hanging, then tuck the ends of the paper clips under ceiling tile beams.

Shower Curtains *

Materials:

- clear shower curtain with a colorful design

Directions:

Create light-filled spaces by hanging the shower curtain between different areas of the classroom.

Variations:

Let children draw their own designs with permanent markers on a transparent shower curtain liner.

Six-Pack Plastic Rings *

Materials:

- plastic rings from six-pack drink cans
- scissors
- yarn or twist ties

Directions:

Punch holes in all four corners of several plastic six-pack rings with scissors. Tie the six-pack sections together with yarn, twist ties, or pipe cleaners. Hang from a wall or ceiling and attach children's work with clothespins.

Variations:

Give children different colors of yarn or ribbon to weave through the rings.

Invisible Walls

Materials:

- 2" x 4" lumber
- hammer, nails

Directions:

Frame areas of the room with 2" x 4" lumber to create open, yet separate interest areas.

Netting

Materials:

- net fabric
- paper clips

Directions:

Hang the net from the ceiling with paper clips to create a special space. Attach natural objects (leaves, vines, flowers) to the net, or decorate with holiday or seasonal art.

Variations:

Hang a fish net from the ceiling and attach children's work with clothespins.

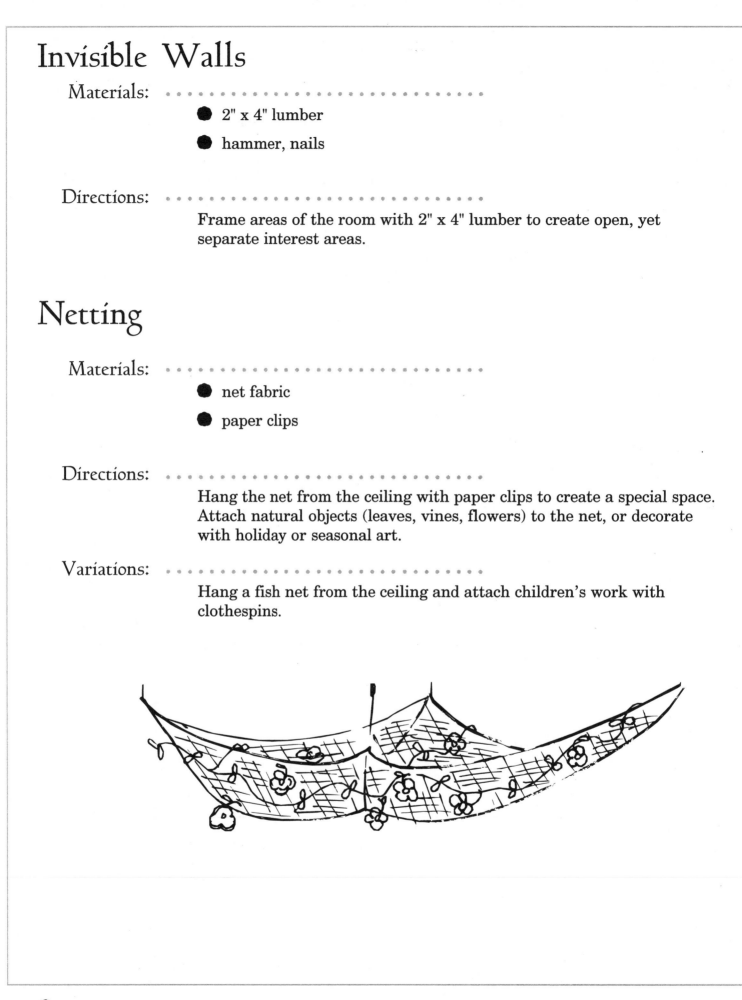

Window Treatments

Curtains, shades, and valances all soften a room and give it a home-like atmosphere.

Roman Shades

Materials:

- butcher paper
- paint and paintbrushes
- tacks, tape, or stapler
- ribbon

Directions:

Cut the butcher paper as wide as the windows and three feet long. (If windows are wider than the butcher paper, make several smaller sections and tape them together.) Let the children spatter paint by throwing it at the paper. Tape or tack one end of the paper to the top of the window frame. Roll the bottom end and loosely tie it with two ribbons.

Variations:

Make similar curtains by stapling fabric to the top of the window. Tie up with ribbons.

Cardboard Cornices

Materials:

- solid or juvenile print fabric
- cotton batting
- glue gun
- heavy cardboard or foam board
- scissors, hammer, nails

Directions:

Cut pieces of cardboard 8" deep and the width of the windows plus 4". Glue cotton batting to the front of the cardboard. Cut the fabric 14" wide and the width of the window plus 8". Cover the cardboard and padding with the fabric, then glue in place in the back. Nail panels to the top of the windows.

Swags

Materials:

- fabric (double the width of the windows)
- ribbon
- tacks

Directions:

Center the fabric and tack it to the top of the window frame. Gather up fabric in the corners and tie with a ribbon.

Variations:

Make rubberband puffs at the corners.

Crumple butcher paper and use to create swags.

Borders

Borders tend to tie a room together. Adapt colors, shapes, and fabrics to blend in with your room.

Materials: ....

- heavy fabric, wallpaper, or children's art
- scissors
- border pattern
- tape or sticky-tack

Directions: ....

Measure the walls in the room. Select a fabric, wallpaper, or art project that you like. Use the pattern below to cut out enough pieces to go around the room. Use sticky-tack or tape to hang it near the ceiling.

Variations: ....

Bulletin board borders or contact paper can be used in a similar manner.

Let children color or paint on adding machine rolls and use for borders.

Hint: Small checks, stripes, solids, polka dots, plaids, and tiny prints work well. Avoid large, complicated designs.

Dive In Pools

These pools will give children a defined place to play and create cozy spaces in the classroom.

Materials:

- plastic swimming pool
- pillows, quilt
- books

Directions:

Place the pool in a quiet area of the room. Fill the pool with pillows, a quilt, and books. Let several children at a time "dive in" and read.

Variations:

Add writing materials, Legos, play dough, and other manipulatives to the pool.

Take the pool out onto the playground and make a quiet area where children can read and relax.

Box It

Boxes invite children to use their imaginations, and they create wonderful props and little spaces for play.

Materials:

- large corrugated cardboard boxes (appliance boxes work well)
- utility knife*
- masking tape
- paints, markers, crayons

Directions:

Ask the children to suggest things they could make out of the boxes. Cut out doors and windows with a utility knife, then let the children decorate the boxes with markers, crayons, paints, and their imagination.

Variations:

Divide children into small groups; give each group a large box, and let them design their own houses. They can paint the outside, wallpaper the inside, and add other details.

* Keep knife out of children's reach.

Bag It

Create a center full of bags and pocketbooks that children can fill and carry around.

Materials:

- pocketbooks
- billfolds
- cloth bags
- change purse
- briefcase
- keys
- small suitcase
- basket
- paper bags with handles
- paper and pencils
- toys and goodies (vary for the age of the children)

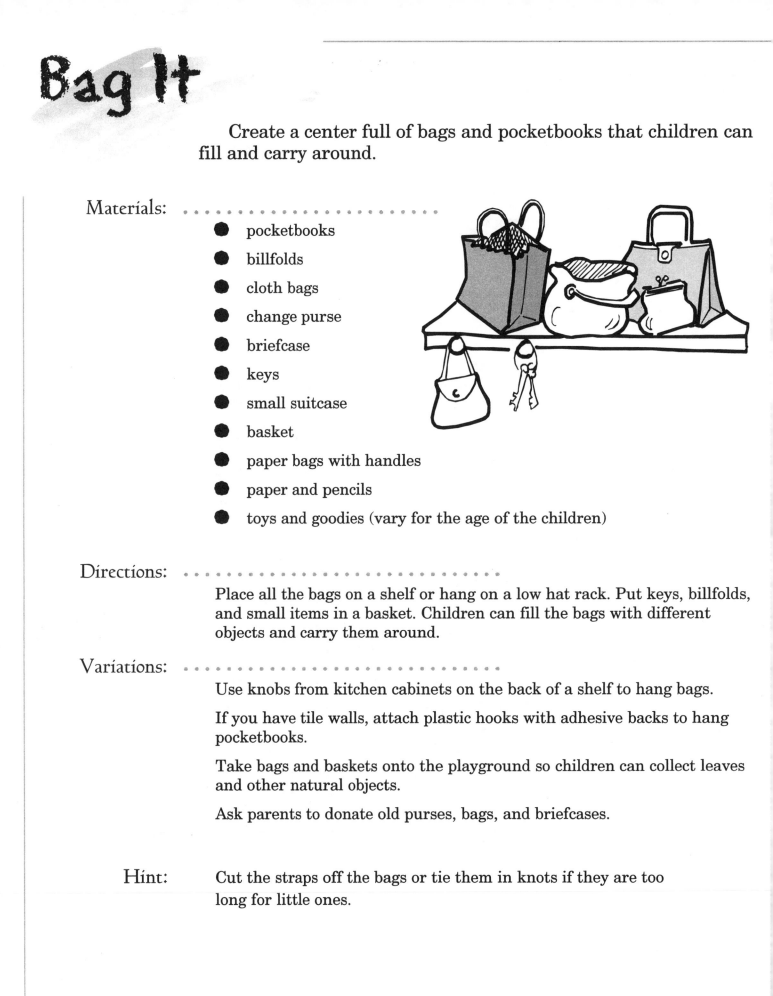

Directions:

Place all the bags on a shelf or hang on a low hat rack. Put keys, billfolds, and small items in a basket. Children can fill the bags with different objects and carry them around.

Variations:

Use knobs from kitchen cabinets on the back of a shelf to hang bags.

If you have tile walls, attach plastic hooks with adhesive backs to hang pocketbooks.

Take bags and baskets onto the playground so children can collect leaves and other natural objects.

Ask parents to donate old purses, bags, and briefcases.

Hint:

Cut the straps off the bags or tie them in knots if they are too long for little ones.

Help Yourself Pockets

A shoe bag can be a handy way to display materials and create learning centers. It can be hung from the back of a shelf, a door, a wall, or even on a playground fence.

Materials:

- clear plastic shoe bags
- art materials
- writing materials
- natural objects
- toys

Art Pockets

Use shoe pockets to hold art materials such as scissors, glue, crayons, markers, tape, yarn, paper scraps, collage materials, and recycled objects. Hang near a table so children can help themselves while creating pictures and sculptures. For outdoor art carry the shoe bag out onto the playground and hang it on a fence near a picnic table.

Writer's Nook

Fill shoe pockets with pens, pencils, sticky notes, envelopes, different kinds of paper, and stamps.

Science Surprise

Place a magnifying glass, magnet, prism, field guide, nuts, bones, shells, leaves, and other interesting objects in the pockets.

Toy Bag

Put cars, trucks, dolls, rattles, small balls, and other age-appropriate toys in the bag.

Music, Music

Display rhythm sticks, bells, shakers, and other instruments in pockets.

Hint: Shoe bags can be cut in half to create two centers.

Texture Board

Children will enjoy exploring these different textures, and they'll be challenged to identify them with their eyes closed.

Materials:

- large poster board
- glue
- various textures such as cotton, peanut shells, rice, gravel, feathers, corrugated cardboard, Styrofoam packing, contact paper (sticky side), satin, burlap, bubble wrap, aluminum foil, yarn, sandpaper, macaroni, and confetti

Directions:

Glue small samples of the textures onto the poster board. Hang the poster board on the back of a shelf or door. Have the children touch the different objects and describe how the objects feel.

Variations:

Ask the children to close their eyes and identify the different textures.

Glue textures to index cards. (Make two of each texture.) Let children spread them out and try to match them up with their eyes closed.

Take texture cards out onto the playground and see if the children can find similar textures in nature.

Felt Board Fun

Flannel boards allow children to use their imaginations, practice language skills, and extend classroom concepts. Flannel boards can be used independently or with small and large groups of children.

Class Flannel Board

Materials:
- felt (cut to fit the bulletin board)
- stapler
- felt pieces cut in shapes of animals and story figures
- Velcro

Directions:

Staple the felt to the bulletin board. Attach Velcro (hook side) to the backs of the felt pieces. Give children the opportunity to tell stories to friends, using the felt pieces as illustrations.

Variations:

Staple colorful fabric to the top of the bulletin board and then drape it to the sides so it looks like a theater stage.

Tape Velcro to the backs of pictures or photographs and use them on felt boards.

Cut out felt geometric shapes and math counters.

Individual Flannel Boards

Materials:

- empty fabric bolts (free from fabric store)
- glue
- felt (cut to go around fabric bolts)
- felt pieces

Directions:

Glue felt around the fabric bolts to make individual flannel boards. Give children small felt pieces in story shapes to use on their flannel boards.

Variations:

Glue felt to 8½" x 11" pieces of corrugated cardboard to make small felt boards.

Attach felt to one side of a cookie sheet with double-sided carpet tape to make a felt board. Use the other side for magnetic pieces.

All Around the Room

Materials:

- felt
- double-sided carpet tape

Directions:

Tape felt to the side of a desk or file cabinet, or to the back of a shelf, to take advantage of unused space.

Variations:

Give children magnetic pieces (letters or pictures with magnetic tape on the back) to use on a file cabinet or metal door.

Glue felt to one side of a metal cookie sheet. Children can use one side with felt pieces, and other side with magnetic pieces.

Bubble

What a unique environment you will create within your classroom with this bubble — and think of all the possibilities it can have used with a theme or unit!

Materials:

- 2 plastic painting tarps (9' x 12')
- 1 roll duct tape
- 1 box fan (ask parents to lend an old one)

Directions:

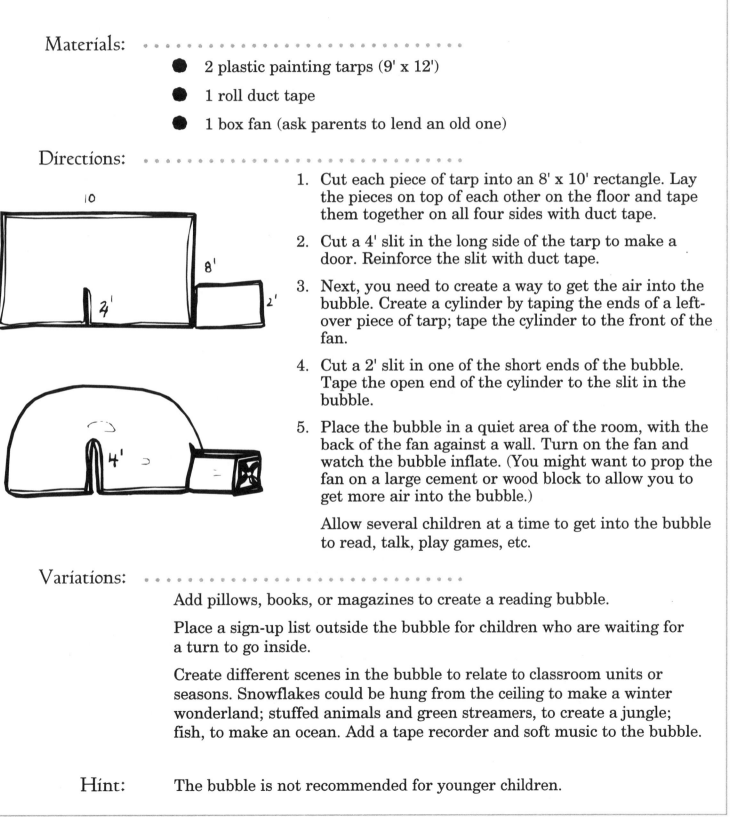

1. Cut each piece of tarp into an 8' x 10' rectangle. Lay the pieces on top of each other on the floor and tape them together on all four sides with duct tape.

2. Cut a 4' slit in the long side of the tarp to make a door. Reinforce the slit with duct tape.

3. Next, you need to create a way to get the air into the bubble. Create a cylinder by taping the ends of a left-over piece of tarp; tape the cylinder to the front of the fan.

4. Cut a 2' slit in one of the short ends of the bubble. Tape the open end of the cylinder to the slit in the bubble.

5. Place the bubble in a quiet area of the room, with the back of the fan against a wall. Turn on the fan and watch the bubble inflate. (You might want to prop the fan on a large cement or wood block to allow you to get more air into the bubble.)

   Allow several children at a time to get into the bubble to read, talk, play games, etc.

Variations:

Add pillows, books, or magazines to create a reading bubble.

Place a sign-up list outside the bubble for children who are waiting for a turn to go inside.

Create different scenes in the bubble to relate to classroom units or seasons. Snowflakes could be hung from the ceiling to make a winter wonderland; stuffed animals and green streamers, to create a jungle; fish, to make an ocean. Add a tape recorder and soft music to the bubble.

Hint: The bubble is not recommended for younger children.

A Touch of Nature

Nature has a calming effect, so bring the outside in with these ideas.

Beauty ·

Display plants and flowers in the classroom. Grow seeds and cuttings.

Animals ·

Classroom pets are fun to observe, and children can develop responsibility from caring for them.

Investigation ·

Place leaves, seeds, grass, flowers, dirt, snow, and other natural objects in a water table for exploration.

Art ·

Paint with sticks, pine needles, and flowers. Let children glue natural objects onto cardboard and paper plates to create a collage.

Math ·

Give children nuts, leaves, flowers, and rocks to sort, count, add, and make patterns.

Science ·

Rotate natural objects in the science area. Encourage children to bring interesting things they find at home to add to the collection.

Concept Basket ·

Take a basket outside and challenge the children to find all the green things they can on the playground. On returning to the classroom, spread them out and sort, count, etc. (Find objects that have different shapes, objects that are soft, objects that are yellow, etc.)

Bird Watching

Children of all ages will get into bird watching with this feeder outside your classroom window.

Materials:

- clear vegetable oil bottle
- scissors, hole punch
- wooden stick
- birdseed
- field guide to birds
- 2 cardboard rollers
- string, tape, pipe cleaner

Directions:

Make a bird feeder from the vegetable oil bottle by cutting windows in the sides. Insert a stick in the bottom for a perch, fill with birdseed, and tie onto a tree near a classroom window with the pipe cleaners. Make binoculars from the cardboard rollers. Place the binoculars and bird identification book near a window where children can see the feeder. The children can then try to identify the birds they see at the feeder in the book.

Variations:

Ask children to do a weather watch and draw what the weather is like outside the window.

Give the children real binoculars. Encourage them to be world watchers and look for all the animals, plants, people, or other objects they can see outside the window.

Play Trays

Lunchroom trays give children a defined area in which to work. Further, they get children involved in materials that are often forgotten on shelves.

Materials:

- lunchroom trays (available at restaurant supply stores)
- manipulative toys
- sensory materials

Directions:

Place two to four trays on a table with materials similar to the ones below:

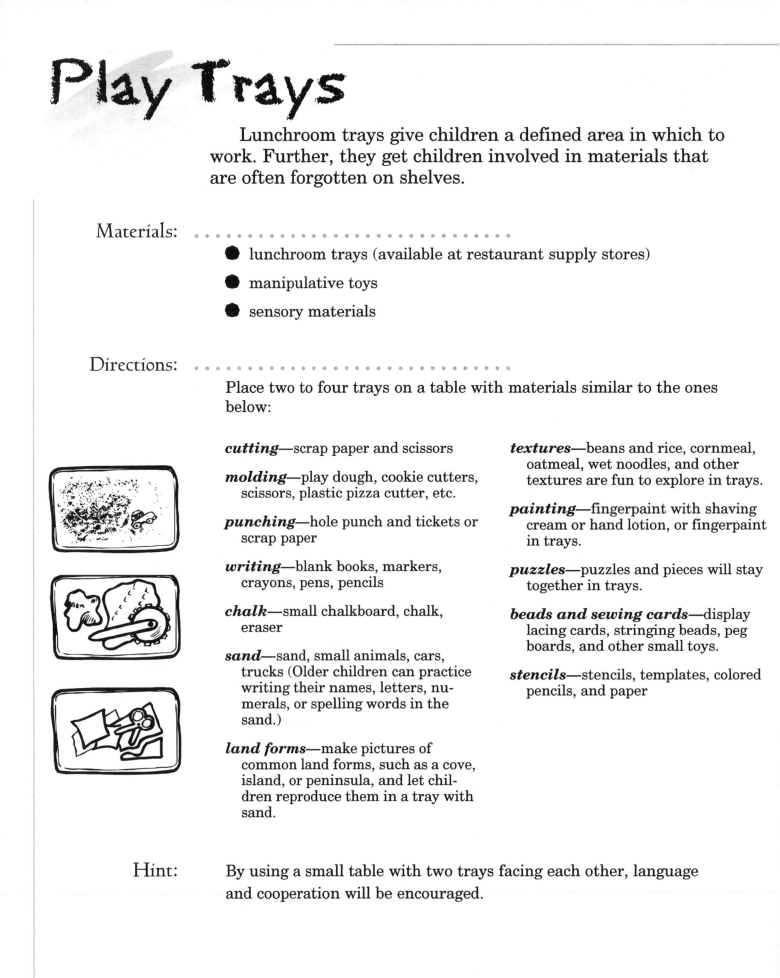

cutting—scrap paper and scissors

molding—play dough, cookie cutters, scissors, plastic pizza cutter, etc.

punching—hole punch and tickets or scrap paper

writing—blank books, markers, crayons, pens, pencils

chalk—small chalkboard, chalk, eraser

sand—sand, small animals, cars, trucks (Older children can practice writing their names, letters, numerals, or spelling words in the sand.)

land forms—make pictures of common land forms, such as a cove, island, or peninsula, and let children reproduce them in a tray with sand.

textures—beans and rice, cornmeal, oatmeal, wet noodles, and other textures are fun to explore in trays.

painting—fingerpaint with shaving cream or hand lotion, or fingerpaint in trays.

puzzles—puzzles and pieces will stay together in trays.

beads and sewing cards—display lacing cards, stringing beads, peg boards, and other small toys.

stencils—stencils, templates, colored pencils, and paper

Hint:

By using a small table with two trays facing each other, language and cooperation will be encouraged.

Puppet Theater

Puppets are a magical way for children to express their thoughts, feelings, and imaginations. Puppets also encourage social skills, problem-solving, and language development among children. This puppet theater will provide children with a special way to act out stories, songs, rhymes, and real-life situations.

Materials:

- large appliance box
- utility knife*
- fabric
- glue
- markers or paints

Directions:

Cut a hole in one side of the box to be the stage of the puppet theater. (An adult will need to do this.) Cut a door in the back of the box so children can get into it. Glue a fabric ruffle to the top of the stage. Let the children decorate the box with markers or paints.

Variations:

Use a tension curtain rod and old curtain across a door frame to create a puppet theater.

Let children make tickets for their puppet shows and invite other classes to their performances.

Tie in puppet productions with literature, themes, songs, or celebrations.

* Keep knife out of children's reach.

Puppets, Puppets, Puppets!

Here are some delightful puppets children will enjoy creating and using in the puppet theater.

Sock Puppet
Let children decorate old socks with markers, buttons, yarn, wiggly eyes and other art supplies to create puppets they can wear on their hands.

Stick Puppets
Have children cut animals or characters out of construction paper and glue them to craft sticks.

People Puppets
Cut people out of magazines or catalogs and staple them to straws.

Hanger Puppets
Stretch a coat hanger into a diamond shape. Pull the leg of an old pair of hose over the hanger and knot at the bottom. Decorate with paper scraps, felt, wiggly eyes, buttons, yarn hair, etc.

Envelope Puppets
Recycle used envelopes by cutting them in half. Decorate with markers or crayons; insert your fingers in the opening.

Spoon Puppets
Use wooden ice cream spoons to make puppets by drawing on them with fine tip markers.

Dinosaur Puppets ·

Cut a 7" slit up the back of a rubber glove. Make spikes for the dinosaur by cutting zigzags in a 7" x 3" piece of felt. Staple the felt in the slit in the glove; draw a face with markers on the middle finger as shown.

Sack Puppets ·

Decorate lunch sacks with construction paper scraps, crayons, markers, and collage materials to create puppets.

Paper Plates ·

Staple two paper plates together ¾ of the way around. Draw on the plates with markers or crayons; insert your hand into the opening.

Glove Puppet ·

Cut the fingers off an old glove; decorate with markers, felt scraps, or wiggly eyes to make worms, insects, or little people.

Cardboard Roller ·

Decorate a toilet paper roll with markers, paints, or construction paper to make puppets.

Finger Puppets ·

Cut out small characters from paper and glue them to 2½" strips. Wrap the strips into circles, tape, and wear them around the finger.

Busy Boxes

Busy boxes are a convenient way to store self-contained activities that can be used by individual children or small groups of children. They're perfect for entertaining children who arrive early or those who can't settle down at naptime. You can also use them to enhance learning centers by rotating props in the block area, adding collage materials in the art center, or for adding props in the dramatic play area.

Busy boxes can be made from shoe boxes, detergent boxes with handles, plastic tubs, or empty ice cream gallons. Cover the cardboard boxes with contact paper or spray-paint to make them more attractive. Also, label the boxes with words and picture cues.

Mail Box
Fill with junk mail, paper, envelopes, pens, and pencils.

Punch and Snip
Add a hole punch, scissors, and scrap paper.

Math Kit
Put in manipulatives to sort and count, a ruler, minute timer, play money, paper, and pencils.

Sewing Box
Add beads, buttons, straws, and pasta (with holes) to string on yarn, shoelaces, ribbon or string. Burlap, plastic needles, yarn, and sewing cards can also be used.

Animal Safari
Put in zoo animals, arctic animals, farm animals, and berry baskets for cages.

Let's Go
Small cars, trucks, planes, boats, and road signs will keep children zooming.

Grab Bag Art
Fill with paper scraps, recycled junk, collage materials, crayons, glue, scissors, etc.

Writer's Kit
Add blank books, envelopes, sticky notes, stamps, notepads, pencils, pens, and markers.

Game Time
A deck of cards, concentration cards, dice, or dominoes can be stored in a box.

Play Dough Factory
Give children cookie cutters, a plastic pizza cutter, scissors, textured objects, toy dishes, plastic wrap and a plastic knife to play with the dough.

Puppet Pals
Fill a box with finger puppets, stick puppets, or hand puppets.

Dress Me
Put in an old shoe and shoelace, zipper, buttons, and snaps (cut-off old garments), and buckles (cut 10" from old belts and punch holes).

My Puppy
Children will have fun playing with a stuffed dog, grooming brush, leash, plastic bowl, empty food container, dry dog biscuits, dog toys, etc.

Jewelry Box
Add costume jewelry, old watches, scarves, mirror, hair bows, and gloves.

Concept Boxes
Collect objects beginning with a certain sound, objects of a like color, or objects of a like shape.

Odds and Ends
Keys, wind-up toys, music boxes, a kaleidoscope, and other objects will interest children.

Story Box
Put in a book and puppets or toys for acting out the story.

Baby Box
Fill a box with a baby doll or stuffed animal, clothes, blanket, bottle, and other baby items.

Making Music
Add musical instruments and other things that can be used to make noise.

Sports Bag
Tennis balls, sponge balls, beach balls, a jump rope, bean bags, visor, and pom poms can be used in a sports bag.

Picture Box
Fill a box with pictures from magazines, calendars, toy catalogs, photographs of the children, or family photos.

A Quiet Place

There will be times when children need to be alone to think, relax, release emotions, or gain self-control. The "Quiet Place" provides children with an area where they can have privacy and peace.

Materials:

- large box lined with pillows or carpet squares
- wooden loft
- bean bag chair
- stuffed chair
- plastic cube lined with pillows
- small tent (drape a blanket over a table)
- cloth tunnel
- tape with classical music

Decorate a large appliance box to look like a doghouse or clubhouse. Put carpet squares on the floor and add pillows or books.

Pull a shelf away from a wall to make a cozy corner. Add a beanbag chair, pillow, stuffed animal, and a mirror.

Drape a large scarf or piece of fabric between two shelves to create a "dream center." Add pictures of peaceful places and pillows.

* The Quiet Place should be limited to one or two children at a time.

Portfolio Place

Portfolios provide ongoing assessment and are a way to document how children are developing and how they use skills. Portfolios show what children can do, and give a more inclusive view of different areas of growth.

Materials: . . . .

- file folders
- photographs of children
- glue, scissors
- markers, crayons
- plastic crate

Directions: . . . .

To make portfolios, glue each child's picture to the top of a file folder. Let the children decorate the outside of their portfolios with markers or crayons. Store the portfolios in a plastic crate in a convenient place in the classroom and label it "Portfolio Place." Encourage the children to file pictures or stories they write in their portfolios. Other items that can be included in portfolios are:

self-portraits

art projects

writing samples (scribbles, name, journal)

work samples (math, group projects, motor activities)

anecdotal records (funny sayings, special moments)

photographs

dictated stories

teacher observations

tapes of children talking or reading

summary of parent conferences

Hint: Date all items in portfolios, then use them to communicate with parents at conference time.

Sharing Box

This idea will eliminate some of the confusion of show and tell, while helping children learn to share with their classmates.

Materials:

- toys, books, and objects children bring from home
- large box

Directions:

Involve the children in decorating the box with paints, pictures, markers, or crayons. Write "Sharing Box" on the outside. When children bring toys or books to school, ask them to put them in the box as they walk in the door. Designate a time when children can get out their things and informally share them.

Variations:

Have special themes for "show and tell." For example, children could be asked to bring in a sign of fall, a picture of their grandparents, something they have made, something that is purple or something that starts with the letter "M". (Integrate this with teaching units or skills.) Label a shelf or table where children can place the objects they have brought in.

Family Culture Box

These boxes will celebrate the families in your classroom,
while providing children with a meaningful multicultural activity.

Materials:

- boxes with a lid

- postcards, books, clothes, cooking items (empty boxes), games, toys, travel brochures, ethnic restaurant menus, audiotape, artwork, etc.

Directions:

Ask parents and children to donate some of the above objects or other items that reflect their culture. (Explain that the children will be playing with these things, so do not include anything valuable.) Put the objects in a box with the child's name and the culture represented by the objects. Let individual children share their culture boxes with classmates. Leave the box open for free exploration, or put various objects in centers around the room. For example, cooking utensils and food boxes could go in the dramatic play area, books in the library, or a tape in the music center.

Variations:

Compare the items in different culture boxes. How are they alike? How are they different?

Ask parents to read a book to the class in their native language. (They could also make a tape.)

Ask parents to send in a picture of a family celebration. Put the pictures in a scrapbook for children to look at.

Play With Me

(Home/School Learning Tasks)

This is an exciting way to involve parents in extending their children's learning at home with fun projects and quality time.

Materials:

- library pockets or envelopes cut in half
- poster board
- markers, scissors, glue
- 3" x 5" index cards

Directions:

Write each child's name on a library pocket or envelope. Print "Play with Me" on the poster board, then glue the pockets onto the poster board as shown. Write a different activity children can do at home with their parents on each index card. (Use the suggestions on the following page, or make up your own to reflect your children's abilities and interests and your curriculum). Send a note home to your parents about the learning tasks that their child will bring home each week. Remind parents to have fun with their child as they do the activity, and to return the card by the end of the week. Place a different card in each child's pocket at the beginning of each week, and follow up with parents about how they are enjoying the activities.

Variations:

Number the activities and keep a graph to help with recordkeeping.

Make a vacation fun pack for families with the activities on the following page. Run off copies of the activities, then cut them up and put the strips in a can or box that the children have decorated. Tell the children that they can pick something special to do from the can each day they are on vacation.

Home/School Activities

1. Take a walk together.
2. Say your phone number and address.
3. Help fold the laundry.
4. Count the doors in your home.
5. Look for something beautiful outside.
6. Can you find ten things in your house that are red?
7. Read a book together.
8. Put on some music and make up a dance.
9. Find a picture in a magazine and make up a story about it.
10. Draw foods you like on a paper plate.
11. Can you hop, skip, gallop and jump?
12. Say some nursery rhymes.
13. Practice what you would do if there were a fire at your house.
14. Find eight objects that are smaller than your thumb.
15. Teach a song to your family.
16. Think of words that rhyme with "man," "cat," "like," "big," "hot," and "bee."
17. Cook something for your family to eat.
18. Go on a shape hunt around your house; find squares, triangles, and circles.
19. Play a game like "Hide and Go Seek" or "I Spy."
20. Name the months in the year.
21. Draw a picture for someone you love.
22. Go outside at night. What can you see in the sky? What sounds do you hear?
23. If you had three wishes, what would you wish for?
24. Find something that starts with b, m, s, f, l, r, and h.
25. Plan a party or special outing for your family.
26. Give a back rub to someone in your family.
27. Say "Please" and "Thank You" all day.
28. How many canned foods do you have in your kitchen?
29. Make a paper sack puppet.
30. Say some jokes or funny riddles.

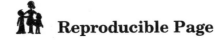 **Reproducible Page**

Top Ten Storage Tips

Teachers are packrats by nature, but these storage tips will eliminate clutter and improve organization.

1. Toss it in the trash. If you don't use it anymore, get rid of it!

2. Purchase clear plastic storage containers. Try to select boxes that you can stack on top of each other. Label the contents on the end of each box. (If you use cardboard boxes, spray-paint or cover them with contact paper so they all look alike.)

3. Hide messy shelves and cabinets with curtains, murals, or posters. Use tablecloths to hide stored objects under a table, such as in the science center.

4. Group like objects together in a logical place where they are used. File materials by month, teaching themes, content areas, etc.

5. Rotate toys, books, and materials. When children are no longer interested in something, put it away and get out something new.

6. Put bulletin boards in garbage bags, then hang them on skirt hangers in a closet. (Store language experience charts and posters in the same way or use a garment bag.)

7. Pizza boxes, plastic tubs, Ziploc bags, plastic crates, clear food containers, detergent boxes, and shoe boxes can all be used for storing art supplies and manipulatives. Label each with the word and picture.

8. Put toys and art supplies on low shelves where children can reach them. Take the time to teach children how to care for materials and clean up after themselves. (Teacher materials should be kept on high shelves or in closets.)

9. Put odds and ends and bits and pieces that you don't know what to do with on the art table for the children to use in collages and sculptures.

10. Do a major clean-up at the end of each month. After several weeks of looking at the same bulletin board or display, children have generally lost interest in it.

Classroom Rating Scale

Use this classroom rating scale to help you determine your strengths and weaknesses. Make goals for improvement based on the areas indicated below.

	Almost Always	To Some Extent	Needs Improvement
Children are generally happy and excited about coming into your classroom			
Children are actively engaged in activities and rarely wander around			
Children interact cooperatively with each other and seldom argue			
Most of the pictures and displays in the classroom are made by the children			
Language experience stories and other examples of print are utilized			
The classroom reflects cultural diversity with books, posters, toys, and other bias-free materials			
Family photographs are displayed			
There are places where children can be alone			
Soft elements are included in the classroom, i.e., rugs, pillows			
Learning centers and shelves are labeled			
Children can make choices about where they want to play			
There are opportunities for large group, small group, and independent learning			
There is a balance of active and quiet times			
Children play outside daily			
Children are given large blocks of time (45 minutes to an hour) to engage in learning centers			
Children can get out and put away materials independently			

 Reproducible Page

	Almost Always	To Some Extent	Needs Improvement
There are at least four choices of activities in each learning center			
The classroom is neat and free of clutter			
Materials are rotated in the different learning centers to maintain interest			
Dramatic play and other areas are integrated with units of study			
Plants, animals, and natural objects are used in the classroom			
There is an open art area so children can create on their own			
Different learning styles and abilities are provided for			
There is enough space for children to move around and work freely			
Children can work independently with little adult supervision			

PART 3

Creating A Literate Environment

Children should be immersed in language so they can begin to appreciate its beauty and importance at an early age.

This section will show you how to use labels, signs, and language experience charts in your classroom in meaningful ways. Suggestions for making books, a creative alphabet, and rebus activity cards will also be presented.

Signs

Signs can be used to encourage reading and writing skills, to demonstrate how functional language is, and to remind children of appropriate behavior.

Put a reminder on the back of the bathroom door

Use a sign to show where riding toys should be parked.

Use signs on the classroom door to show where you are.

Create bilingual signs

Charts and Posters

Use charts and posters daily to reinforce the usefulness of reading and writing.

Sign In

Let each child draw her face on a circle and attach it to a popsicle stick. As the children come into the classroom each day, have each child select her stick from a basket, then place it in an envelope with her name on it. (Real photos of the children's faces can also be used.)

Job Chart

Write jobs on a poster, then write children's names on cutouts of hands. Attach Velcro to the backs of the hand cutouts and the poster so that each child can put his name by the job he would like to do.

Daily Schedule

Write your daily schedule on a poster. Illustrate with real photographs of children participating in these activities or with pictures from school supply catalogs. (Use a clothespin to mark your progress through the schedule as you complete different activities.)

Song Chart

Let children tell you their favorite songs and write them on a poster. Add a picture clue for each song. When you need a song, ask a child to choose one from the chart.

Songs and Poems

Write words to songs, poems, or finger plays on charts. Point to the words as the children say or sing them.

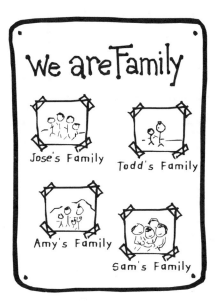

Family Photos

Display photos of children's families.

Grandparents

Ask children to bring in pictures of their grandparents. Hang them on a poster and label.

Language Experiences

Language experience charts reinforce the concept that, "What I say can be written down, and what is written down I can read."

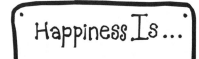
Happiness Is...

Tasha - Spending the night with Granny.

Josh- Riding my bike.

Sami- Getting my new bird Tweetie.

Beth- My birthday party!

Complete a sentence
Ask children to complete an open-ended sentence.

The Pumpkin Patch

We went to Farmer Joe's Pumpkin Patch.

We rode a big yellow Bus.

We had a picnic.

Field Trip
Follow up a field trip with a story about it.

Message Board

Don't forget!

Messages
Use a message board with sticky notes as a reminder to you and the children.

Unit of study
Relate language experience charts to a unit of study.

When I Grow Up

Sadik - I might be a fire fighter.

Maria - I want to be a doctor.

Fritz - I'm going to be a baseball player.

Cutouts

Write children's individual responses to questions on cutouts, then tape them onto a door.

Class Rules

Let children help formulate classroom rules. Refer to the rules when there is a conflict.

cLass Rules

Be kind to Friends.

Take care of yourself.

Take care of our things at School.

Today's Special

Write a message to the children each morning welcoming them. Include the special activities you will do that day.

GOOD MORNING Friends!

What a great day we will have!

We're going to read a story about monkeys,

then make a monkey sandwich.

Star Student

Highlight unique qualities of a different child each week. Include her picture, likes, dislikes, favorite books, pets, etc.

Linesia Ray

Star **Student**

Linesia is five years old.

She likes to read and roller skate.

She has two little brothers.

Pink is her Favorite Color.

Daily News

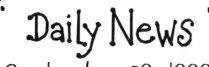

September 29, 1999

We went to a puppet show in the library.

We sorted leaves,

then we made party pizzas for snack.

We played ponies outside.

Daily News

At the end of the school day, have the children recall the events of the day in sequence. Write down what they liked best or what they learned.

Homework

Write down a homework assignment or extension activity children can do each evening. Have the children read over it with you before they leave each day.

HOMEWORK

Bring in a sign of Fall.

Don't forget to bring in old newspapers for the paper drive.

Rebus Activity Charts

Rebus cards encourage children to "read pictures," follow directions, and work independently.

Magic Pennies

You will need:
Vinegar
Salt
Cup & Spoon

Directions:
1. Fill the cup half way with water.
2. Add 3 spoons of salt.
3. Stir the pennies.
4. Taa Daa! Shiny Pennies!

Science Experiments

Place directions for science experiments on charts.

Music

Have children construct their own musical instruments.

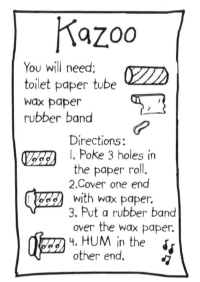

Kazoo

You will need:
toilet paper tube
wax paper
rubber band

Directions:
1. Poke 3 holes in the paper roll.
2. Cover one end with wax paper.
3. Put a rubber band over the wax paper.
4. HUM in the other end.

Glue Globs

You will need:
Glue
Paper plate
Food coloring

Directions:
1. Put a glob of glue on the plate.
2. Add a drop of red, yellow and blue food coloring.
3. Slowly turn the plate around.

Art Projects

Hang directions for art activities in the art center.

Cereal Necklace

You will need:
cereal
yarn
tape

Directions:
1. Cut a peice of yarn.
2. Put tape around the end
3. String cereal on the yarn.
4. Tie the ends together.

Manipulatives

Children will develop motor skills as they follow picture directions.

Cook's Nook

Children will enjoy preparing their own snacks with rebus recipe cards. Reading, math, and self-help skills are all reinforced as children cook.

Materials:

- large chart tablet, markers
- cooking utensils
- food

Directions:

Prepare recipe and snack charts similar to the ones below and on the next page. Carefully explain the directions, serving sizes, clean-up procedures, safely precautions, etc. Allow children to work independently or in small groups as they cook their snacks. (Younger ones will need adult help.)

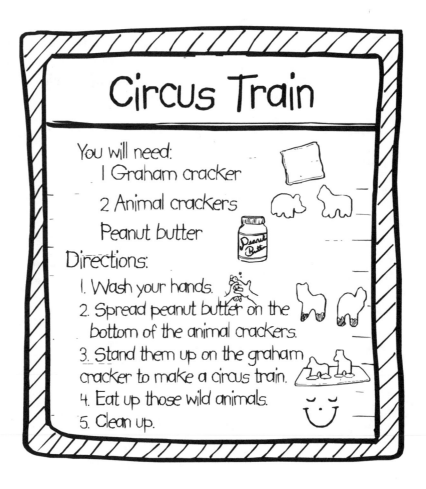

Spider Snack

You will need:
1 round cracker
6 raisins
8 pretzel sticks
peanut butter

Directions:
1. Wash your hands.
2. Spread peanut butter on the cracker.
3. Make a face with the raisins.
4. Add 8 pretzels for legs
5. Clean up!

Monkey Tail Sandwich

You will need:
1 banana
1 hot dog bun
peanut butter

Directions:
1. Wash your hands.
2. Spread peanut butter in the bun.
3. Peel the banana and put it in the bun.
4. Yum! yum!
5. Clean up!

Letters, Letters, Letters

Famous People ....

Write letters to the President, Governor, movie stars, etc. (You can get their addresses at the library.) Frame the letters you receive from famous people.

Thank You's ....

Write thank-you notes after field trips or to thank guest speakers. School helpers and parent volunteers will also appreciate notes of thanks.

Teacher Mailbox ....

Make a mailbox from a cereal box and encourage the children to write you letters.

Student Mailboxes ....

Make a mailbox for each child from clasp envelopes and staple them onto a bulletin board or tape them to children's cubbies.

Junk Mail ....

Give children junk mail to play with. (Most parents will be glad to send in their junk mail, too.)

Story Box

Stories will come alive for children as they retell them with a story box. This is a great way to extend literature and encourage language development.

Materials:

- school box, cigar box, or other box with a lid attached
- felt, felt scraps
- scissors, glue
- favorite books or folk tales

Directions:

Cut felt to fit on the inside lid of the box and glue it in place. Using felt scraps, cut out the main characters and props from one of the books. Place the book and felt characters in the box, then decorate the outside of the box with a picture and the book title. Read the book to the class and demonstrate how to use the figures inside to retell the story. Place the story box in the library so the children can use it with friends.

Variations:

After children have practiced retelling the story, let them take home the story box and share it with their families.

Invite parents in for a workshop and have them make story boxes for the classroom.

Write Ideas

Official Report ....

Take a spiral ring notebook and write "official report" on it. When a child starts to tattle or complain, hand him the book and tell him to "write it down."

**Newspaper
Report** ....

When children go on a field trip, assign one child to be the reporter and to write down what the children do and see.

Turns List ....

Keep a clipboard with paper and pencils by favorite classroom activities. Children can sign their names to indicate they are waiting for a turn. (You can also use a "turns list" on the playground for riding toys, swings, etc.)

Graphs ....

Integrate language and math skills with graphs.

Wipe-Off Boards

Writing skills will flourish when children are provided with individual wipe-off boards.

Materials:

- 8' x 4' sheet of wipe-off board (available at building supply stores)
- dry erase markers
- permanent magic marker
- plastic crate or box

Directions:

Cut the wipe-off board into twenty sections. (They will usually do this where you purchase the board.) Using the permanent marker, print each child's name at the top of a board in dotted lines. Place the boards in a crate or box for children to use independently. They can practice writing their names, draw pictures, write words, etc.

Variations:

Have each child bring in an old sock to use as an eraser.

Attach a wipe-off board to the wall of a classroom or hall for the children to use for writing or drawing.

Use the boards for learning games. Have the children sit on the floor with their boards in their laps. Ask them to reproduce shapes, make sets, write numerals, etc. Older children could write spelling words, math facts, etc.

Stuff an empty cereal box with newspaper, then cover with white contact paper. Children can write on the white contact paper with Crayola water soluble markers, then erase with a wet towel.

Hint:

Only dry-erase markers can be used on wipe-off boards.

Labels

Before children read words, they read pictures. Picture and word labels reinforce reading concepts, and enable children to be independent and clean up after themselves.

Materials:

- school supply catalogs
- poster board or construction paper
- glue, scissors
- markers

Directions:

Make a list of different toys, supplies, and materials in your classroom. Cut pictures of those objects from school catalogs. Glue the pictures to small pieces of poster board or construction paper and print the words beside the pictures. Tape these labels to shelves, cabinets, boxes, and other objects.

Variations:

Attach labels to shelves with clear contact paper.

Use pictures from the boxes toys come in to make labels.

Let the children draw their own pictures of toys and supplies to use on the labels.

Trace around objects on black paper and use the silhouettes to label shelves.

Create labels for learning centers that include pictures, a list of skills children develop from playing in the center, and the number of friends who may play there.

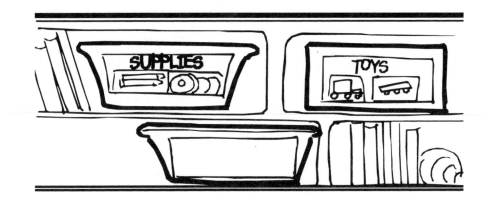

Letter and Number Land

This is a meaningful, hands-on way to introduce children to letters and numerals.

Materials ·

- poster board cut in 8" x 10" rectangles
- markers
- glue gun
- small classroom objects and toys for each letter of the alphabet

Directions: ·

Print a letter of the alphabet in the upper left corner of each card. Glue an object that begins with the sound of that letter on the card with the glue gun. (Involve the children in finding these objects in the classroom. For example, you could use a plastic apple for A, a block for B, a crayon for C, a toy dog for D, an eraser for E, a feather for F, etc.) Let the children write the name of each object on the bottom of the card as shown. Hang the letters up around the classroom at the children's eye level.

Variations: ·

Use children's names and photographs to make alphabet cards. (Take pictures of other people or objects in the school for letters if you don't have children's names.)

Make an alphabet of environmental print by gluing labels, logos, and other familiar words to poster board.

Purchase inexpensive party favors to use in making number cards. Write the numeral on the card, then glue on that set of objects. Let the children write the words.

Hint: Put a border around the outside of each card with a magic marker.

Walk-About Story

All children will be motivated to read the walk-about story.

Materials: . . . .

- butcher paper
- markers, crayons, or paints
- clear packaging tape

Directions: . . . .

Roll out a long sheet of paper.

Mark off 2' sections on the paper.

Let each child draw his picture and write his name in one of the sections.

Write the following chant in each section:

(First name), (name) who do you see?
I see (second child's name) looking at me.

(Second name), (name) who do you see?
I see (third child's name) looking at me.

And so forth....

Tape the paper to the floor with clear packaging tape. (You can also cover it with clear contact paper.)

Variations: . . . .

Let the children write and illustrate their own original stories using a similar format.

Have the children work together to write and illustrate a story. Hang the pages in the hallway. Tape a sheet of paper to the top of each page so other students walking down the hall will be curious and will want to lift the sheets and read the story.

Steppin' Out a Story

Children will begin to identify important elements in a story as they physically "step it out."

Materials: . . . .
- construction paper (different colors)
- markers
- clear contact paper

Directions: . . . .

Cut the construction paper into different large shapes. Write one of the following elements of a story on each of the construction paper shapes: title, character, setting, problem, and solution. Place the shapes on the floor and cover with clear contact paper. After reading a book to the children, let them stand on the different sections to identify the various parts of the story.

Variations: . . . .

The construction paper may also be laminated and taped to the floor.

Adapt the elements to the age and ability of the children. For older children you might include the author, illustrator, beginning, middle, and end of the story.

Homemade Books

Making books with children not only utilizes their reading and writing skills, it also encourages their creativity and problem-solving ability. Furthermore, children are motivated to read the books that they and their classmates write. These homemade books can be a great addition to your classroom library; children can also take them home and share them with their families.

Photo Album Books

Purchase inexpensive photo albums with magnetic sheets. Use children's drawings, stories, or photographs to make books in the albums.

Class Books

Give each child a piece of paper and ask him to write a story or draw a picture relating to a specific topic. (It might be about a unit of study, a field trip, holiday, school event, favorite person, what the children want to be when they grow up, wishes, their families, feelings, etc.) Staple the children's pages inside construction paper and decorate the cover. After reading these books to the class, let different children take them home to share with their families.

Cereal Box Book

Ask the children to save their empty cereal boxes and bring them to school. Cut the front covers off the boxes. Punch two holes in the top of each box, then attach them with book rings. Children can "read" the different brands of cereal. (Other food boxes, from crackers, cookies, or macaroni, can also be used to make books.)

Tag Along Books

Fold white paper (8½" x 11") inside construction paper (9" x 12") and staple along the fold. After the children have drawn pictures or written stories in these books, punch two holes along the fold. Insert a pipe cleaner in the holes and form a handle. Children can carry around their "tag along" books.

Sheet Protector Books

Put children's drawings or stories in sheet protectors. Attach several sheet protectors with ribbon or yarn to make a book. (Newspaper articles and magazine pictures can also be put in sheet protectors to make books.)

Lunch Sack Books

Take five paper lunch sacks and fold over the bottom of each sack to make a peek-a-boo flap. Draw a picture under each flap so only part of it shows. Staple the lunch sacks together on the left side. Children can try to identify the pictures, then lift the flaps to confirm their guess. (Magazine pictures or cutouts can also be used to make lunch sack books.)

Creative Covers

Staple plain paper between wrapping paper, wallpaper, funny papers, contact paper, maps, stiff fabric, cardboard, food boxes, or other materials to make books.

Grocery Sack Big Books

Cut the front and back off large paper grocery sacks to make pages. Have the children each paint or draw a picture on one of the pages, then dictate a sentence about their picture. Punch holes in the sides and tie the pages together with yarn or string. (Songs, nursery rhymes, and poems are fun to use to make these Big Books.)

Shape Books

Cut construction paper and writing paper into unusual shapes and staple to make books to motivate children to write and read. Geometric shapes, seasonal patterns, animals, or objects that relate to a unit of study can all be used.

Sentence Strip Book

Let the children cut out pictures from school supply catalogs. Glue the pictures to sentence strips, then write sentences children dictate or allow them to write their own sentences to go with the pictures. Punch a hole in the left side of each sentence strip and attach them together with a book ring.

Baggie Book

Cut construction paper to fit inside Ziploc sandwich bags. Glue photographs of the children onto the paper and write a sentence about each of them. (Children can also draw their own pictures, or you can cut out pictures from magazines to make baggie books.) Place the pictures in the baggies and zip shut. Poke two holes in the left side of each baggie, then tie them together with pipe cleaners or bread ties. (Large bags can be used to make bigger books.)

Celebrating Children's Art

Children's art is the most refreshing, original, and charming in the world, and should be the focus of any school environment.

Rather than patterned projects and dittoes where everyone's work looks the same, children need open-ended activities that allow them to think, experiment, problem-solve, and express themselves in unique ways. Art should be process-oriented, for children enjoy the moment and are not concerned with the final product. Since art is the child's outward expression of her inner world, it can also be an emotional release and can provide a vehicle for the development of thinking processes.

- **With art, there is no failure, but simply the joy of the experience.**
- **With art, there should be no comparison, for whatever the child creates is his or hers and should be cherished.**
- **With art, all children can experience success and grow!**

Why would you hang a commercial poster, cartoon character, or plastic cardboard animal drawn by an adult when you can hang an *original* — a one-of-a-kind by a very special child in your school? You'll find you will enjoy looking at the children's art much more than art by an anonymous adult, and the children will, too!

Art Gallery

Displaying children's art attractively reflects the importance of their work.

Artist's Canvas

Materials:

- artist's canvas (available at craft and art shops)
- paints, brushes
- collage materials

Directions:

Let small groups of children plan how they would like to paint the canvas. (Car painting, string painting, gadget prints, sponge prints, tissue collage, glue painting, and body prints are a few ideas.) Encourage the children to give a title to their canvas, then label the picture along with the artists' names.

Variations:

Photograph the children in the process of creating their canvas and display the photo beside the finished product.

Purchase large picture frames and rotate children's paintings in them.

Arrange several plastic box frames on a wall. Rotate children's stories and drawings in the frames.

Pedestals

Materials:

- plastic crate, stool, or cardboard box
- 1–2 yards of velvet, satin, taffeta, or other fabric

Directions:

Drape the fabric over the crate, stool or box in loose folds. Display sculptures or 3-dimensional projects on the pedestal.

Variations:

Stand up puppets made by children on a detergent bottle to display them.

Use an artist's easel to display different projects and paintings.

Display Case

Materials: ....

- lighted display case

Directions: ....

A lighted display case in the lobby of the school will create immediate interest and provide a mini-museum where you can focus children's work.

Variations: ....

Attach jewelry boxes, shoe boxes, or cigar boxes together with tape or glue. Staple these to a bulletin board or nail to a wall to create little shadow boxes in which children can display their projects and treasures.

Plexiglass Gallery

Materials: ....

- sheet of Plexiglass (4'x 8')
- tape

Directions: ....

Drill holes in the Plexiglass and attach it to a wall at the children's eye level. Children can tape their pictures anyplace they want on the Plexiglass.

Hang-Ups

Materials: ....

- clothesline
- clothespins (spring-type)

Directions: ....

Attach the clothesline low on a wall in the classroom or the hallway. As children finish paintings, drawings, or other work, let them hang their pictures on the line.

Variations: ....

Let each child decorate a clothespin with her name. The children can practice identifying their names when they hang up or take down their pictures.

Use the clothesline for learning activities, such as hanging numerals in order or putting letters in alphabetical order.

Four-Sided Display

Materials:

- large appliance box
- paint, paintbrushes
- tape

Directions:

Let the children help paint the box. Tape their pictures to all four sides and display in an open area.

Labeling

Materials:

- index cards
- pens, pencils

Directions:

Have the children dictate how they made their different creations. Post the index cards with their explanations next to their artwork.

Variations:

Older children can write their own descriptions or stories about their art projects.

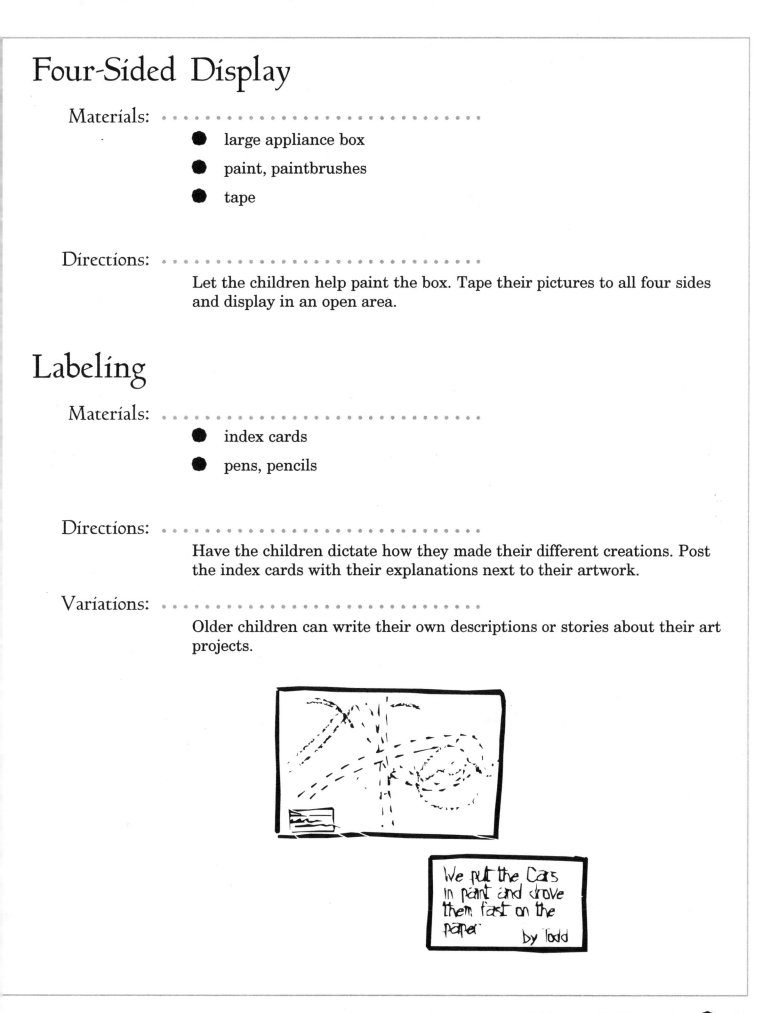

We put the Cars in paint and drove them fast on the paper
by Todd

Marvelous Murals

A mural is a wonderful project that encourages children to work together. Murals can be created with a wide variety of materials, and they provide an interesting focus on classroom walls and hallways.

Relate murals to a unit of study, season, or special interest of the children. Vary paint colors, and experiment with different types of paper and fabric.

When working on murals, hang the paper on the wall, put it on the floor, place it on a large table, or hang it from the playground fence.

Attach labels to murals that tell how children made them, or let the children dictate a story about the process. It's also interesting to take a photograph of the children working on the project to hang by the finished product.

Add borders to murals to create frames; hang the murals at the children's eye level.

Feather Duster Mural

Materials: . . . .

- feather duster
- pie pans
- paint
- butcher paper

Directions: . . . .

Pour the paint into the pie pans. Let the children dip the feather duster into the paint and apply it to the paper.

Variation: . . . .

Give children individual feathers to paint a mural.

Bubble Painting

Materials: . . . .

- bottle of bubbles
- food coloring
- butcher paper

Directions: . . . .

Tape the paper to a playground fence. Add several big squirts of food coloring to the bubbles; blow bubbles on the paper and watch them pop and make designs.

Car Sponge

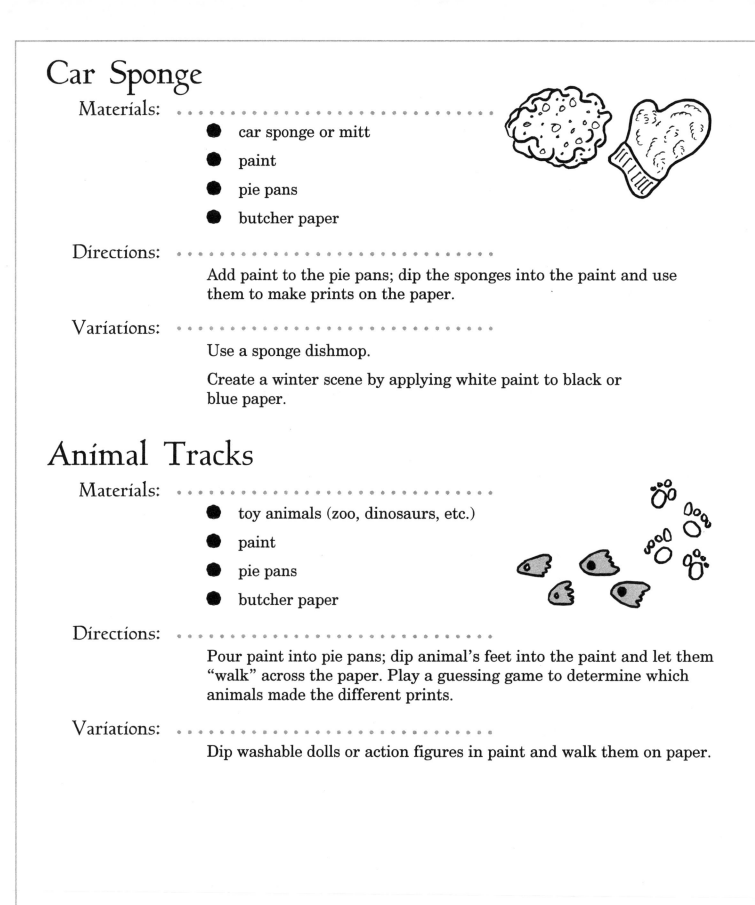

Materials:

- car sponge or mitt
- paint
- pie pans
- butcher paper

Directions:

Add paint to the pie pans; dip the sponges into the paint and use them to make prints on the paper.

Variations:

Use a sponge dishmop.

Create a winter scene by applying white paint to black or blue paper.

Animal Tracks

Materials:

- toy animals (zoo, dinosaurs, etc.)
- paint
- pie pans
- butcher paper

Directions:

Pour paint into pie pans; dip animal's feet into the paint and let them "walk" across the paper. Play a guessing game to determine which animals made the different prints.

Variations:

Dip washable dolls or action figures in paint and walk them on paper.

Let's Go To The Races

Materials:

- toy cars and trucks
- paint
- pie pans
- butcher paper

Directions:

Add paint to the pie pans; dip the wheels of the cars and trucks into the paint and "race" them on the paper.

Variations:

Do you have an old Barbie doll whose head has fallen off? Dip her hair in paint for a unique brush!

Chalk Talk

Materials:

- colored chalk
- cups of water
- butcher paper

Directions:

Dip the chalk in the water, then draw on the paper.

Variations:

Dip chalk in buttermilk or sugar water.

Crayon Bundles

Materials:

- crayons
- rubber bands
- butcher paper

Directions:

Wrap rubber bands around three or four crayons to make bundles. Draw with bundles on the paper.

Variations:

Play music while children draw.

Flower Painting

Materials:

- real or artificial flowers
- paint
- pie pans
- butcher paper

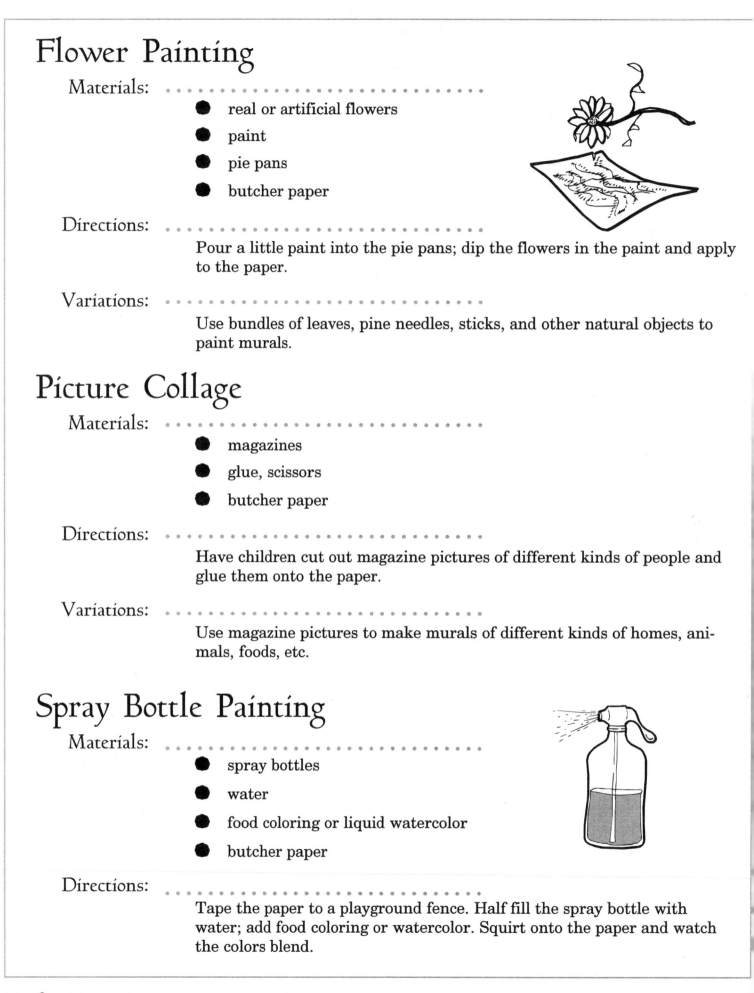

Directions:

Pour a little paint into the pie pans; dip the flowers in the paint and apply to the paper.

Variations:

Use bundles of leaves, pine needles, sticks, and other natural objects to paint murals.

Picture Collage

Materials:

- magazines
- glue, scissors
- butcher paper

Directions:

Have children cut out magazine pictures of different kinds of people and glue them onto the paper.

Variations:

Use magazine pictures to make murals of different kinds of homes, animals, foods, etc.

Spray Bottle Painting

Materials:

- spray bottles
- water
- food coloring or liquid watercolor
- butcher paper

Directions:

Tape the paper to a playground fence. Half fill the spray bottle with water; add food coloring or watercolor. Squirt onto the paper and watch the colors blend.

Fly Swatter Painting

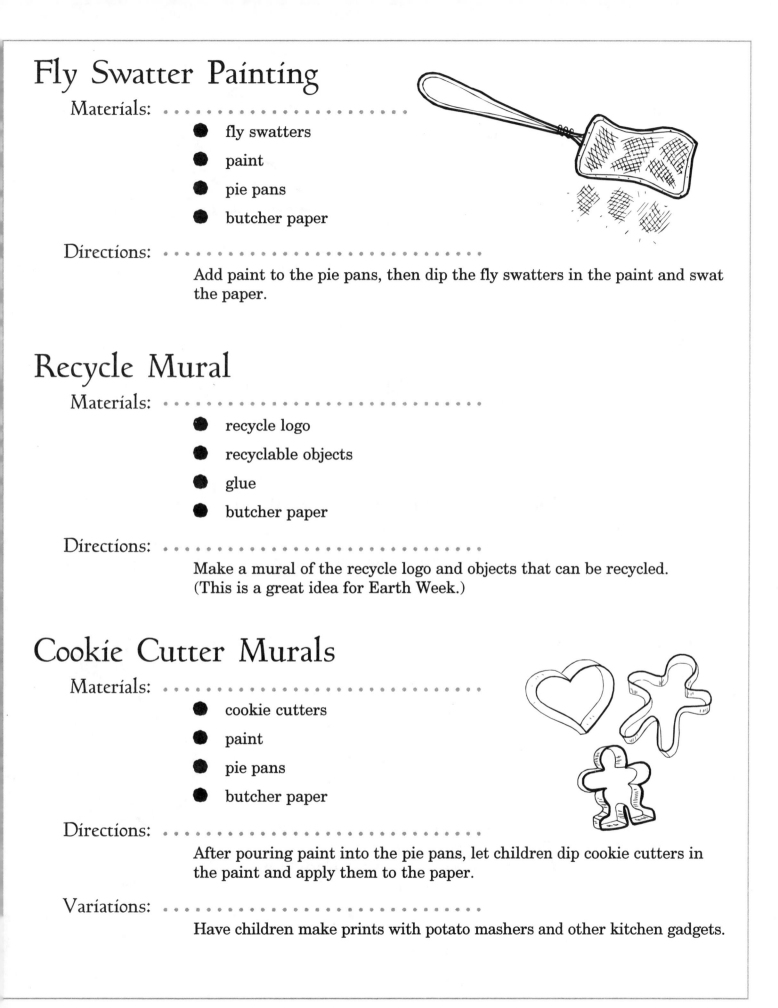

Materials:

- fly swatters
- paint
- pie pans
- butcher paper

Directions:

Add paint to the pie pans, then dip the fly swatters in the paint and swat the paper.

Recycle Mural

Materials:

- recycle logo
- recyclable objects
- glue
- butcher paper

Directions:

Make a mural of the recycle logo and objects that can be recycled. (This is a great idea for Earth Week.)

Cookie Cutter Murals

Materials:

- cookie cutters
- paint
- pie pans
- butcher paper

Directions:

After pouring paint into the pie pans, let children dip cookie cutters in the paint and apply them to the paper.

Variations:

Have children make prints with potato mashers and other kitchen gadgets.

Body Painting

Materials:

- paint
- pie pans
- butcher paper

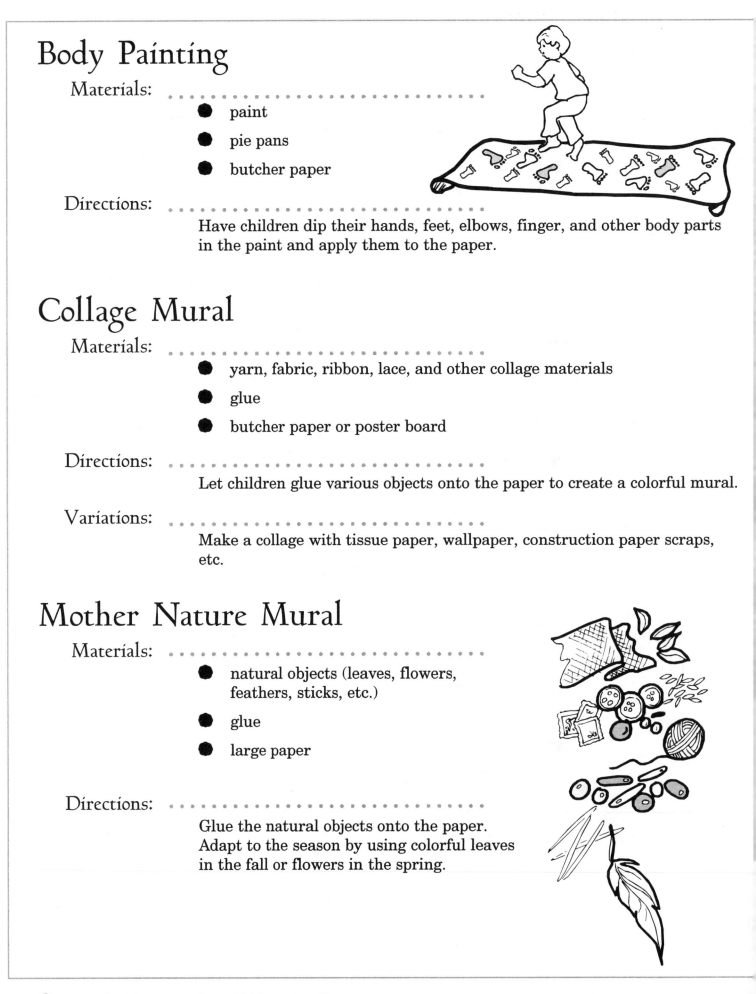

Directions:

Have children dip their hands, feet, elbows, finger, and other body parts in the paint and apply them to the paper.

Collage Mural

Materials:

- yarn, fabric, ribbon, lace, and other collage materials
- glue
- butcher paper or poster board

Directions:

Let children glue various objects onto the paper to create a colorful mural.

Variations:

Make a collage with tissue paper, wallpaper, construction paper scraps, etc.

Mother Nature Mural

Materials:

- natural objects (leaves, flowers, feathers, sticks, etc.)
- glue
- large paper

Directions:

Glue the natural objects onto the paper. Adapt to the season by using colorful leaves in the fall or flowers in the spring.

Shiny Murals

Materials:
- aluminum foil, tinsel, sequins, and other shiny objects
- glue
- large paper

Directions:

Glue the shiny objects onto the paper.

Concept Murals

Materials:
- magazines
- glue
- scissors
- crayons and markers
- butcher paper

Directions:

Have children cut out pictures or draw objects relating to a concept. For example, they could do a "blue mural" with pictures of blue objects. They could also make a mural of objects beginning with a particular letter, or they could cut out pictures of a certain shape.

Rubber Band Brush

Materials:
- rubber bands
- pipe cleaners
- pie pans, paint
- butcher paper

Directions:

String 20 to 30 rubber bands on a pipe cleaner, then twist the pipe cleaner into a handle. Children can dip the rubber bands in paint, then brush them onto the paper.

Flour and Salt Paint

Materials:

- flour
- salt
- tempera paint, brushes
- poster board or heavy paper

Directions:

Mix equal parts of flour and salt. Stir in tempera paint to make a thick consistency. Apply to heavy paper with brushes, fingers or Q-tips.

Postage Stamp Mural

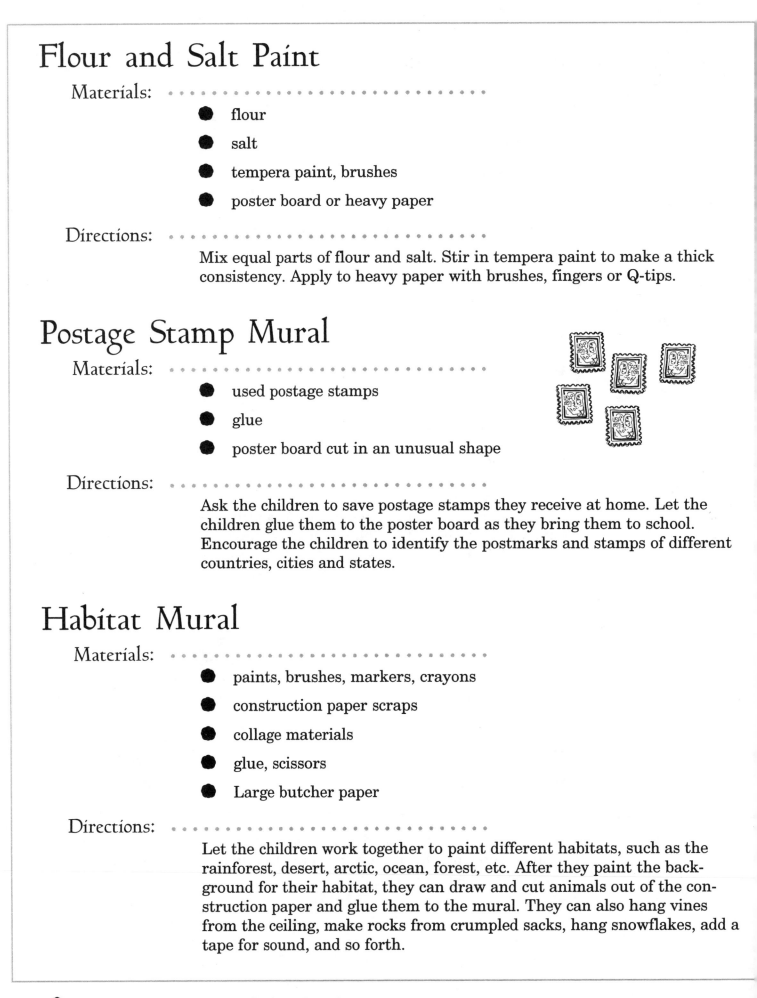

Materials:

- used postage stamps
- glue
- poster board cut in an unusual shape

Directions:

Ask the children to save postage stamps they receive at home. Let the children glue them to the poster board as they bring them to school. Encourage the children to identify the postmarks and stamps of different countries, cities and states.

Habitat Mural

Materials:

- paints, brushes, markers, crayons
- construction paper scraps
- collage materials
- glue, scissors
- Large butcher paper

Directions:

Let the children work together to paint different habitats, such as the rainforest, desert, arctic, ocean, forest, etc. After they paint the background for their habitat, they can draw and cut animals out of the construction paper and glue them to the mural. They can also hang vines from the ceiling, make rocks from crumpled sacks, hang snowflakes, add a tape for sound, and so forth.

Create a Collage

Collages invite children to create, construct, and experiment as they develop small motor skills, plan, and make choices. Collages are always interesting because everyone's is different!

Materials: . . . .

Almost anything that's inexpensive and plentiful can be used to make a collage.

Try some of the following:

rice	used postage stamps	cotton
tissue paper	popsicle sticks	buttons, lace
nuts, seeds	greeting cards	fabric scraps
dried beans	shells	Styrofoam peanuts
magazines, catalogs	cupcake liners	colored sand
toothpicks	wallpaper	fish gravel
pasta	food wrappers	leaves, flowers
brochures	yarn	(colored with
straws	feathers	dry tempera)
wrapping paper	beads	

Collages can be made on:

paper plates	food boxes (cut off front & back)
plastic lids	meat trays
grocery sacks	contact paper
cardboard	
paper (all kinds)	

To attach objects to a collage use:

glue
rubber cement
masking tape
colored glue
  (colored with food coloring)
paste
glue sticks
cellophane tape
liquid starch

Let children tear paper, or use scissors, a hole punch, or precut shapes.

Hint: Limit the number of choices depending on the age of the children.

Put collage materials in clear cartons, muffin pans, butter tubs, or separate containers.

Fabric Collage

Materials:
- fabric scraps
- ribbon, lace, rickrack, buttons, and other sewing notions
- glue, paper

Directions:

Cut up the fabric and arrange it on the paper. Decorate with buttons and other trim.

Variations:

Make a fabric collage on burlap.

Decorate a box lid or oatmeal box with buttons and trim for a gift for Mom.

Letter Collage

Materials:
- poster board
- magazines
- glue
- collage materials

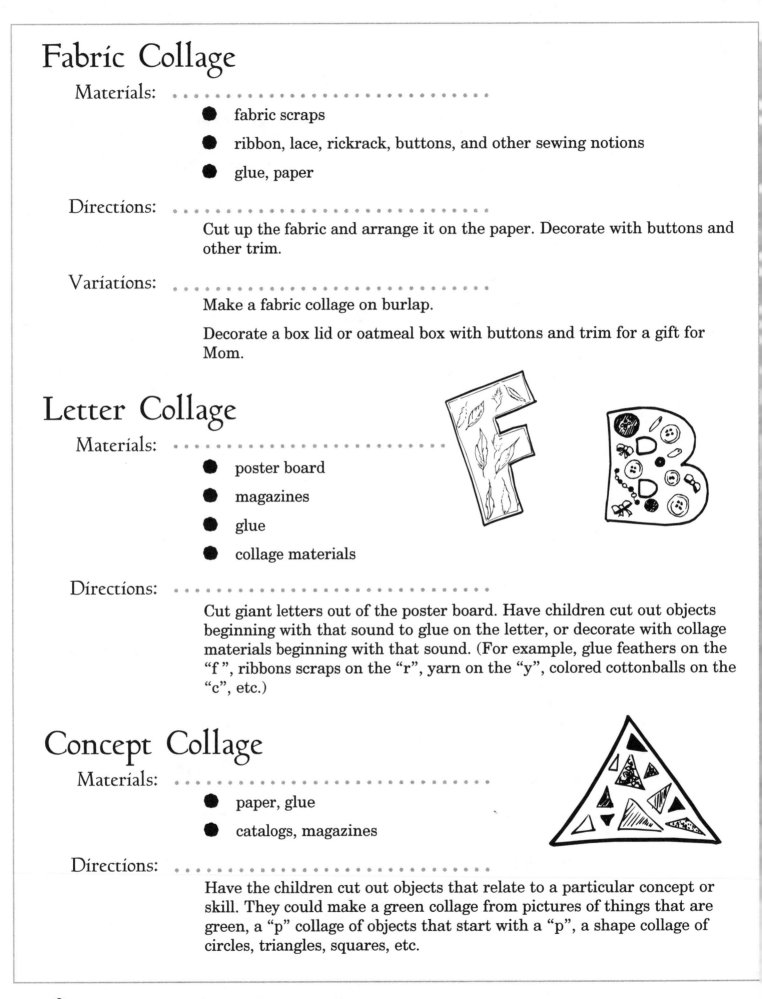

Directions:

Cut giant letters out of the poster board. Have children cut out objects beginning with that sound to glue on the letter, or decorate with collage materials beginning with that sound. (For example, glue feathers on the "f", ribbons scraps on the "r", yarn on the "y", colored cottonballs on the "c", etc.)

Concept Collage

Materials:
- paper, glue
- catalogs, magazines

Directions:

Have the children cut out objects that relate to a particular concept or skill. They could make a green collage from pictures of things that are green, a "p" collage of objects that start with a "p", a shape collage of circles, triangles, squares, etc.

Baggie Collage

Materials:
- Ziploc bags
- tissue paper (variety of colors)

Directions:

Let the children tear tissue paper into small pieces and put the pieces in a baggie. Tape the baggies to a sunny window or staple to a bulletin board.

Variations:

Take the children on a nature walk and let them fill the baggie with leaves, flowers, etc.

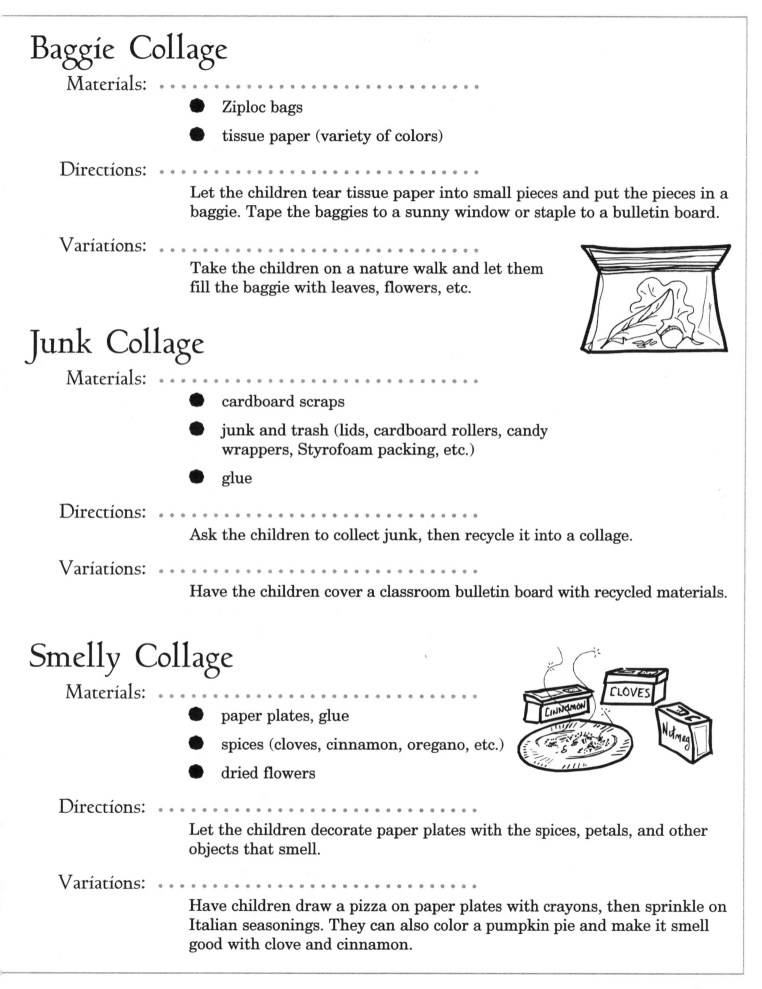

Junk Collage

Materials:
- cardboard scraps
- junk and trash (lids, cardboard rollers, candy wrappers, Styrofoam packing, etc.)
- glue

Directions:

Ask the children to collect junk, then recycle it into a collage.

Variations:

Have the children cover a classroom bulletin board with recycled materials.

Smelly Collage

Materials:
- paper plates, glue
- spices (cloves, cinnamon, oregano, etc.)
- dried flowers

Directions:

Let the children decorate paper plates with the spices, petals, and other objects that smell.

Variations:

Have children draw a pizza on paper plates with crayons, then sprinkle on Italian seasonings. They can also color a pumpkin pie and make it smell good with clove and cinnamon.

Texture Collage

Materials:

- cotton, bubblewrap, velvet, felt, sandpaper, carpet scraps, burlap, and other objects with different textures
- glue
- cardboard scraps

Directions:

Arrange textured objects on the cardboard and glue in place.

Nature Collage

Materials:

- lumber scraps
- glue
- natural objects

Directions:

Take the children on a nature walk to collect leaves, seeds, nuts, small rocks, feathers, moss, and other treasures. Have them glue the objects onto wood scraps.

Variations:

Let children glue natural objects to tree bark, logs, or paper plates.

Vary the nature collage for the season. Create an autumn collage with colored leaves, a winter collage with sticks, dead leaves, and evergreens, or a spring collage with flowers and leaves.

Tissue Paper Collage

Materials:

- tissue paper
- white paper
- spray bottle of water

Directions:

Cut or tear the tissue paper into small pieces, then arrange it on white paper. Spray with water. Dry. Peel off the tissue paper and see the unusual design deposited by the tissue paper.

Variations:

Glue small pieces of tissue paper to wax paper with liquid starch. Dry. Trim the edges and hang from the window as a sun catcher.

Newspaper Art

Using newspapers for art projects is a perfect way to teach children about recycling. In addition to saving money, newspapers provide a large space on which little hands can create.

Pounce Painting

Materials:

- fabric scraps cut in 5" circles
- popsicle sticks
- cotton balls
- rubber bands
- paint
- newspapers

Directions:

Place the fabric on the table and put three cotton balls in the center. Wrap the fabric around the end of a popsicle stick and rubberband in place. Dip in paint, then "pounce" on the newspaper.

Variations:

Tie a jingle bell around the pouncer so it makes noise as you paint. Make pouncers large or small by varying the number of cotton balls.

Put small pieces of sponge in spring clothespins and use as paintbrushes.

Sponge Prints

Materials:

- sponges cut in various shapes
- pie pans, paint
- newspapers

Directions:

Pour a small amount of paint into the pie pans. Let the children dip sponges in the paint, then print with them on the newspaper.

Variations:

Use sponge balls.

Cut sponges into holiday shapes or objects that relate to a theme.

Gadget Painting

Materials:

- plastic berry baskets, toothbrushes, spools, plastic forks, cookie cutters, and other kitchen utensils
- paint, pie pans
- newspapers

Directions:

Put paint in the pie pans. Dip the gadgets in the paint, then print with them on the newspaper.

Variations:

Use pine boughs, sticks, feathers, toy animals, and other objects to print with on newspaper.

Bubblewrap Painting

Materials:

- plastic bubblewrap
- paint, brushes
- newspapers

Directions:

Paint a picture or design on the bubblewrap. Put a sheet of newspaper on top of the bubblewrap and rub. Lift to reveal the design.

Scrap Paper Collage

Materials:

- scrap paper (wallpaper, construction paper, tissue paper, wrapping paper, etc.)
- scissors, glue
- newspapers

Directions:

Cut the scrap paper into different shapes and glue onto the newspaper.

Newspaper Creatures

Materials:

- newspapers
- markers

Directions:

Starting on the fold, tear an abstract shape from the newspaper. Open it up and turn it all around until you see a "creature." Add details with markers or construction paper scraps.

Three-Dimensional Art

Three-dimensional art provides children with a different perspective and challenge.

Clay

Materials: . . . .

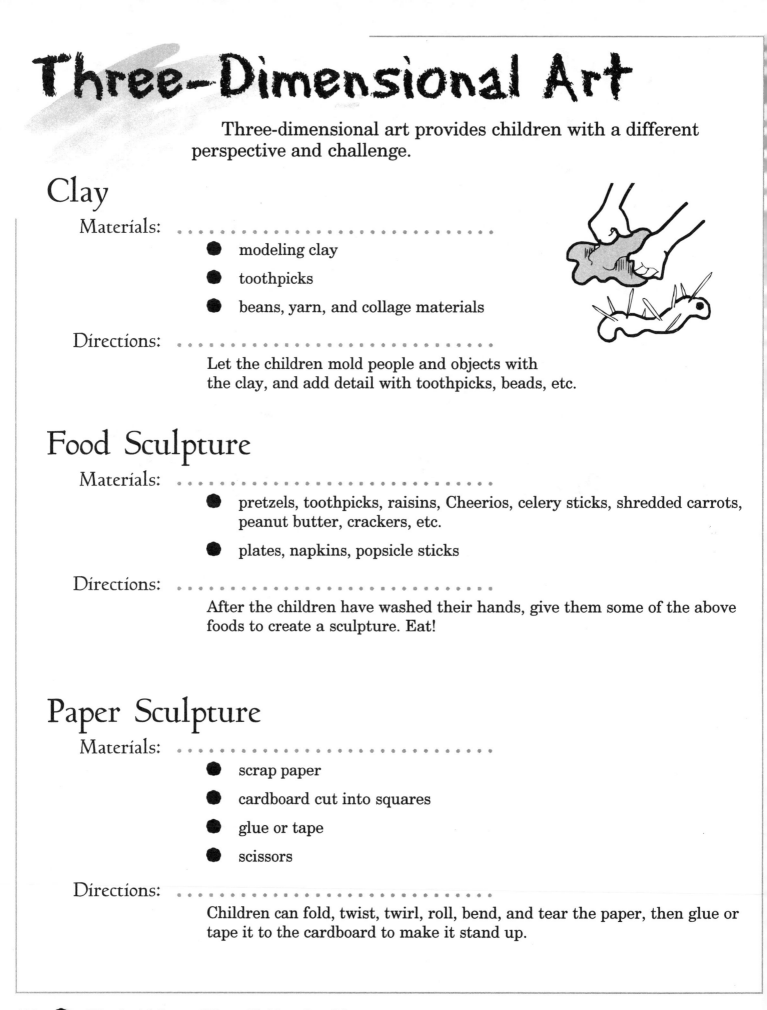

- modeling clay
- toothpicks
- beans, yarn, and collage materials

Directions: . . . .

Let the children mold people and objects with the clay, and add detail with toothpicks, beads, etc.

Food Sculpture

Materials: . . . .

- pretzels, toothpicks, raisins, Cheerios, celery sticks, shredded carrots, peanut butter, crackers, etc.
- plates, napkins, popsicle sticks

Directions: . . . .

After the children have washed their hands, give them some of the above foods to create a sculpture. Eat!

Paper Sculpture

Materials: . . . .

- scrap paper
- cardboard cut into squares
- glue or tape
- scissors

Directions: . . . .

Children can fold, twist, twirl, roll, bend, and tear the paper, then glue or tape it to the cardboard to make it stand up.

Paper Rolls

Materials:
- newspaper or newsprint
- tape

Directions:

Demonstrate how to roll the paper up into tubes. Tape tubes together to make three-dimensional designs.

Variations:

Use funny papers or magazine pages to make paper rolls.

Cardboard Rollers

Materials:

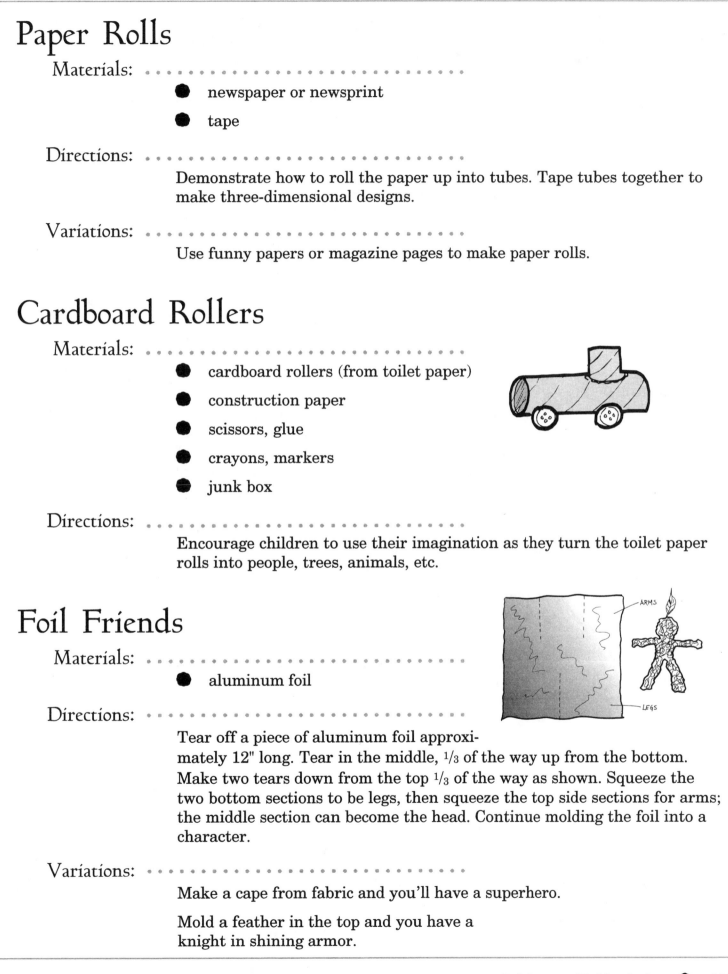

- cardboard rollers (from toilet paper)
- construction paper
- scissors, glue
- crayons, markers
- junk box

Directions:

Encourage children to use their imagination as they turn the toilet paper rolls into people, trees, animals, etc.

Foil Friends

Materials:
- aluminum foil

Directions:

Tear off a piece of aluminum foil approximately 12" long. Tear in the middle, 1/3 of the way up from the bottom. Make two tears down from the top 1/3 of the way as shown. Squeeze the two bottom sections to be legs, then squeeze the top side sections for arms; the middle section can become the head. Continue molding the foil into a character.

Variations:

Make a cape from fabric and you'll have a superhero.

Mold a feather in the top and you have a knight in shining armor.

Styrofoam Creation

Recycle Styrofoam packing into unique sculptures and wall hangings.

Materials:

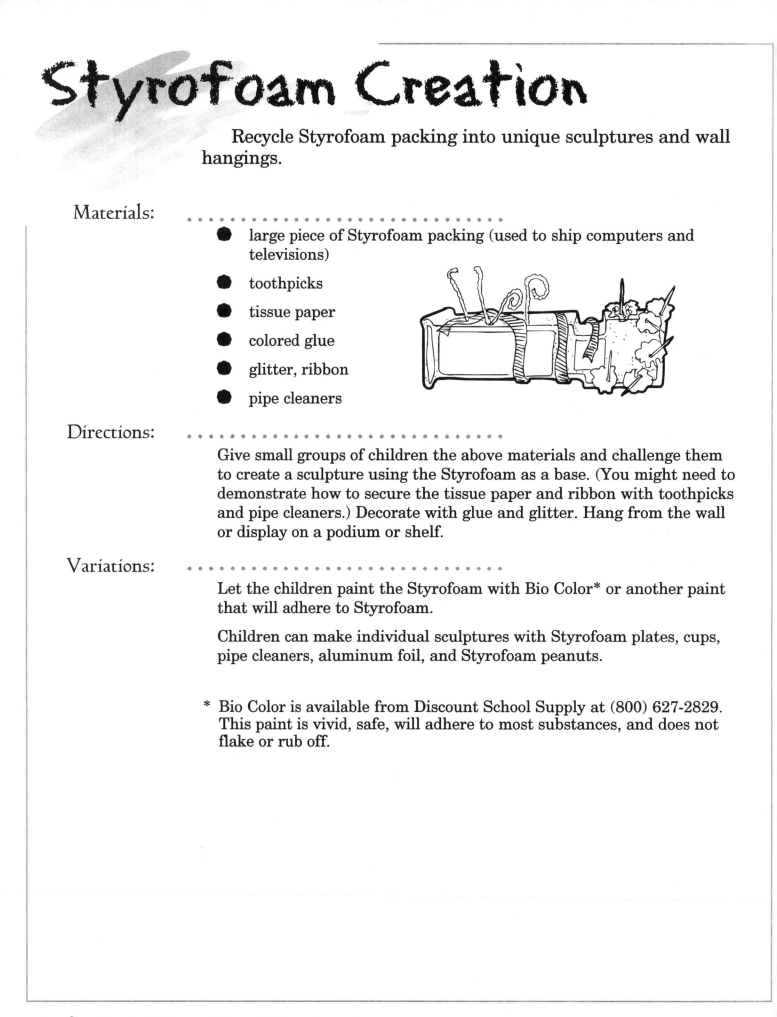

- large piece of Styrofoam packing (used to ship computers and televisions)
- toothpicks
- tissue paper
- colored glue
- glitter, ribbon
- pipe cleaners

Directions:

Give small groups of children the above materials and challenge them to create a sculpture using the Styrofoam as a base. (You might need to demonstrate how to secure the tissue paper and ribbon with toothpicks and pipe cleaners.) Decorate with glue and glitter. Hang from the wall or display on a podium or shelf.

Variations:

Let the children paint the Styrofoam with Bio Color* or another paint that will adhere to Styrofoam.

Children can make individual sculptures with Styrofoam plates, cups, pipe cleaners, aluminum foil, and Styrofoam peanuts.

* Bio Color is available from Discount School Supply at (800) 627-2829. This paint is vivid, safe, will adhere to most substances, and does not flake or rub off.

Moving Sculpture

What an exciting way to involve all the children in your classroom— creating a giant sculpture that is constantly evolving.

Materials:

- corrugated cardboard boxes (any size) — one for each child
- tape
- large paintbrushes (purchase inexpensive ones like painters use)
- red, yellow, blue paint (Bio Color works well, as it does not rub off)
- newspapers
- plastic containers for paint (margarine tubs)
- smocks

Directions:

Ask each child to bring in a cardboard box, or ask an office supply store to save boxes for you. Tape the boxes shut. Cover the working area with newspapers and provide smocks for the children. Pour the paint into the plastic cartons; let each child paint his box with the primary colors. Dry. The next day, encourage the children to paint designs on their boxes. They can also print patterns on them with sponges. Dry. Let the children freely explore building giant sculptures with their boxes. Reinforce what happens when everyone works together.

Variations:

Redesign the sculpture. How tall can they make it? How long? Can they build a tunnel they can crawl under? Can they march around it? Can they think of a title for their sculpture?

Place the boxes in the lobby or hall and let parents, children, and staff move the boxes around.

Play the boxes like drums.

Take them outside on a dry day to play with.

Wall Sculpture

This could go in a real art museum, but children will have fun creating it and seeing it in their school.

Materials:

- foam board
- glue gun
- plastic containers and "junk" (egg cartons, bottles, packages, cake trays, detergent bottles, film containers, beads, old toys, lids, etc.)
- spray paint (must adhere to Styrofoam and plastic)

Directions:

Have children collect the objects and arrange them on the board. Glue the objects in place. (An adult may need to do this with a glue gun.) Spray paint. Hang on the wall.

Variations:

Allow the children to paint the sculptures with paint that will adhere to plastic (i.e., Bio Color).

Glue yarn, tinsel, tissue paper, and other objects to the sculpture after it is painted.

Create a plastic dragon by gluing recycled containers to a strip of felt as shown.

Tube Sculpture

Here's another interesting three-dimensional sculpture.

Materials:
- cardboard rollers (toilet paper, paper towels, etc.)
- paintbrushes
- glue
- corrugated cardboard cut in a geometric shape

Directions:

Let the children paint the cardboard rollers. Dry. Put glue on the bottom of each roller; arrange them on the cardboard to make an interesting design. Display the sculpture on a shelf or hang from the wall.

Variations:

Glue the roller on the cardboard; spray-paint the entire sculpture.

Decorate the rollers with glitter, tissue paper, etc.

Hint:
The sculpture is more interesting if tubes are cut in different lengths.

Sparkle and Shine

Children are attracted by things that glitter and shine, so this project is right up their alley.

Materials:

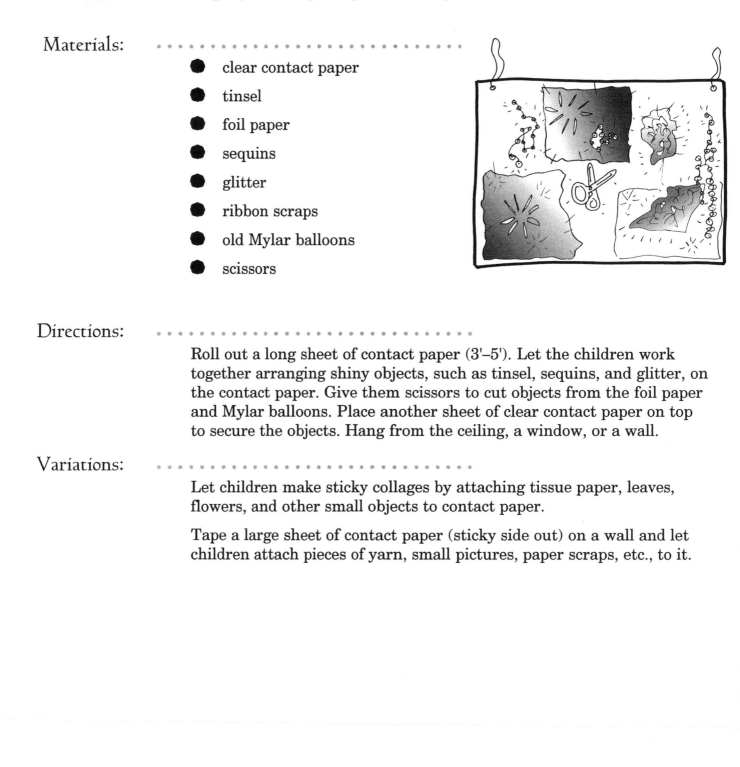

- clear contact paper
- tinsel
- foil paper
- sequins
- glitter
- ribbon scraps
- old Mylar balloons
- scissors

Directions:

Roll out a long sheet of contact paper (3'–5'). Let the children work together arranging shiny objects, such as tinsel, sequins, and glitter, on the contact paper. Give them scissors to cut objects from the foil paper and Mylar balloons. Place another sheet of clear contact paper on top to secure the objects. Hang from the ceiling, a window, or a wall.

Variations:

Let children make sticky collages by attaching tissue paper, leaves, flowers, and other small objects to contact paper.

Tape a large sheet of contact paper (sticky side out) on a wall and let children attach pieces of yarn, small pictures, paper scraps, etc., to it.

Dynamic Dioramas

Dioramas are a unique way for individuals or cooperative learning groups to display their creativity.

Materials: . . . .

- cardboard boxes (shoe boxes for individuals; corrugated cardboard boxes for group projects)
- paper scraps
- paint, paintbrushes
- glue, scissors, tape, string
- pipe cleaners, clay, foil, popsicle sticks, etc.
- collage materials, junk

Directions: . . . .

Ask the children to think of a favorite scene. It could be from a book, a place in their community, a period in history, a celebration, a habitat, etc. Let them paint the inside of the box and create a three-dimensional scene using various art media. Objects can be suspended from the top of the box with string. Stand up characters and props with clay or glue. Characters and animals can be made from paper, clay or papier maché. Natural objects (rocks, sticks, nuts), small boxes, toys, and junk can also be used to build a diorama.

Variations: . . . .

Stack several dioramas on top of each other to create a fascinating display.

Hint: This project can take several days or even weeks to create, so provide children with a place to work and store their dioramas.

The Napping House

Surprise Picture Frame

Children will have fun creating these surprise pictures and making a "surprise" display.

Materials:

- construction paper (2 sheets per child)
- natural objects (seeds, leaves, flowers, feathers, pebbles, shells, etc.)
- glue
- scissors

Directions:

Take the children on a nature walk and let them collect natural objects. (Challenge them to find things that are lightweight.)

Put the natural objects in the middle of one sheet of paper. Take the second sheet and cut diagonal lines out from the middle to within one inch of the corners as shown. Put glue around the edges of the second sheet, then place it on top of the sheet with the natural objects. Take each point and roll it back from the middle around a pencil. (This should make a pop-up frame around the objects.)

Variations:

Stick objects on a sticky sheet of contact paper. Place a curled construction paper frame on top of it.

Mobiles

Mobiles allow children to plan, construct, and experiment with ordinary materials in a unique way. Mobiles also add interest to your classroom.

Coat Hanger Mobile

Materials: . . . .

- coat hangers
- crayons, markers
- scissors, hole punch
- construction paper
- yarn or string

Directions: . . . .

Color and cut out various shapes and objects from the construction paper. Punch holes in the shapes and tie them onto the coat hanger with string or yarn. Hang from the ceiling or light fixture.

Variations: . . . .

Relate mobiles to a season, holiday, theme, or story.

Let children cut out the letters in their name and hang the letters on the mobile.

Earth Day Mobile

Materials: . . . .

- coat hangers
- tape
- string or yarn
- trash (candy wrapper, foil, plastic bags, etc.)

Directions: . . . .

Take the children on a nature walk and let them collect litter and trash. (They can also bring recycled materials from home.) Tape the trash to the coat hanger or tie it on with a string.

Nature Mobile

Materials:

- stick or tree branch
- natural objects (leaves, feathers, shells, seed pods, pine cones, flowers, etc.)
- string or yarn

Directions:

Attach a string to the stick for hanging; tie on the other natural objects.

Spiral

Materials:

- paper plates
- scissors, glue, hole punch
- construction paper scraps
- string or yarn

Directions:

Cut the paper plate into a spiral as illustrated. Cut out objects from the construction paper and tie them onto the spiral with string or yarn. Hang from the center of the spiral.

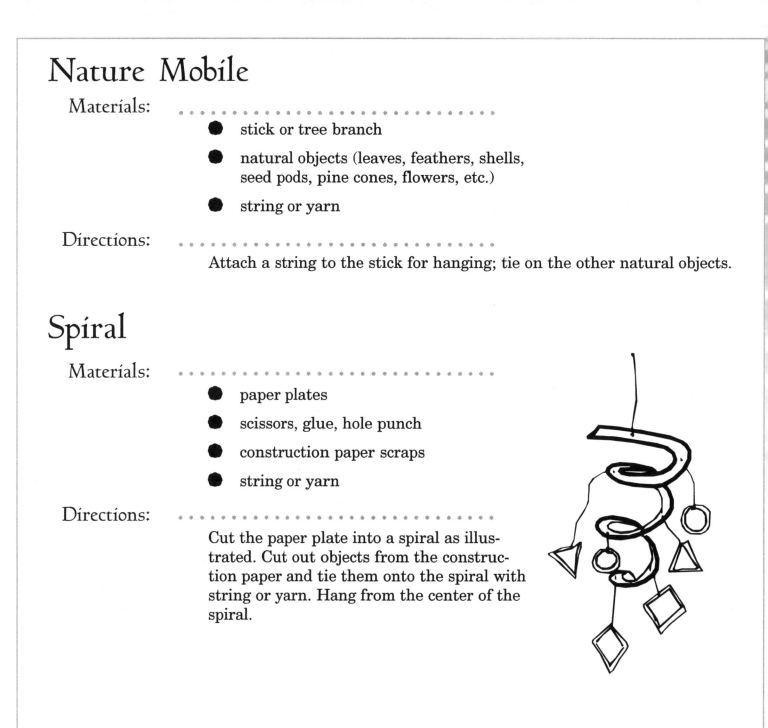

Banners, Banderas, and Windsocks

Halls and rooms can get "hung up" with these ideas.

Banners

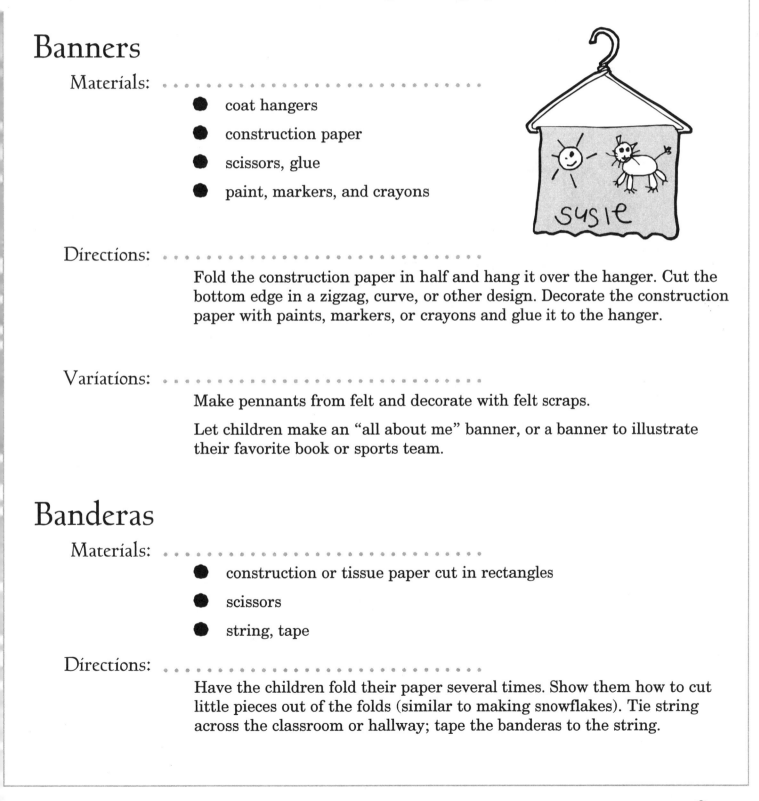

Materials:

- coat hangers
- construction paper
- scissors, glue
- paint, markers, and crayons

Directions:

Fold the construction paper in half and hang it over the hanger. Cut the bottom edge in a zigzag, curve, or other design. Decorate the construction paper with paints, markers, or crayons and glue it to the hanger.

Variations:

Make pennants from felt and decorate with felt scraps.

Let children make an "all about me" banner, or a banner to illustrate their favorite book or sports team.

Banderas

Materials:

- construction or tissue paper cut in rectangles
- scissors
- string, tape

Directions:

Have the children fold their paper several times. Show them how to cut little pieces out of the folds (similar to making snowflakes). Tie string across the classroom or hallway; tape the banderas to the string.

Windsocks

Materials:

- construction paper (10" x 18" rectangles)
- tissue paper
- paints, markers, crayons
- hole punch, scissors
- glue, stapler

Directions:

Decorate the paper horizontally. Turn it over and glue strips of tissue paper (12" x 18" long) to the bottom as shown. Bring the sides together to make a cylinder and staple. Punch three holes evenly spaced on the top edge. Tie a 12" piece of string to each hole; bring the ends of the string together and knot.

Variations:

Make mini-windsocks from toilet paper rolls. Decorate with markers and add tissue paper streamers.

Paper Chains

Paper chains demonstrate connectedness and can be used to reinforce learning while they decorate the classroom.

Materials:

- construction paper cut in strips
- glue or stapler
- crayons, markers

Friendship Chain

Ask each child to decorate a strip of paper with his name and designs. Glue or staple the strips together to make a friendship chain and hang in the classroom.

Countdown Chain

Make a chain using the number of links equal to the number of days left until a vacation, field trip, party, or other celebration. Each day remove a link until the special day arrives.

Diary Chain

At the end of each day, have the children tell you what they liked best or learned that day. Write what they say on a strip of paper and date it. Each day add to the chain and hang it around the classroom as it grows. (You might want to use a different color paper each month.)

Seasonal Decorative

Make chains to decorate the classroom for different seasons or holidays. For example, red, white, and blue could be used in July, or orange and black could be used in October. Hang chains around windows or from the ceiling.

Rainbow Chain

Make paper chains of different colors in the rainbow. Loop them from the ceiling to create a rainbow in the classroom.

Family Chain

Let each family in your school decorate a strip of paper, then create a large chain that represents the entire school.

Crumpled Paper Sculpture

Crumpled paper can be sculpted into trees, animals, and other interesting objects.

Materials:

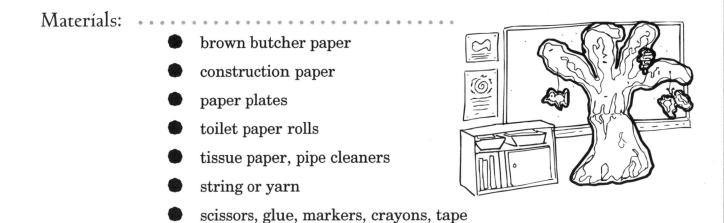

- brown butcher paper
- construction paper
- paper plates
- toilet paper rolls
- tissue paper, pipe cleaners
- string or yarn
- scissors, glue, markers, crayons, tape

Directions:

Crumple the butcher paper several times until it is pliable and can be molded. Sculpt it into a tree trunk with branches, then staple it to a bulletin board or tape it to a wall. Cut leaves or vines out of construction paper and add them to the tree. Make other objects to hang from the branches:

Snakes—Color paper plates, then cut them into a spiral.

Monkeys—Add heads, arms, legs, and a tail to toilet paper rolls to make little monkeys.

Butterflies—Make butterflies by folding 8" squares of tissue paper back and forth. Twist a pipe cleaner around the middle of the fold; ruffle tissue paper to make wings.

Birds—Use construction paper to make birds.

Flowers—Take four pieces of tissue paper cut in 6" squares. Fold back and forth in accordion folds and twist a pipe cleaner around the middle of the folded shape. Separate layers to open into a flower.

Variations:

Mold rocks, mountains, animals, vehicles, homes, or other objects that relate to a season or unit of study out of crumpled paper. Let the children add detail and decorate.

Giant Animals

Children will enjoy working together to make these giant creatures and pretend characters.

Materials:

- butcher paper
- paint, chalk, markers, crayons, or collage materials
- scissors, stapler
- newspaper

Directions:

Lay a piece of butcher paper on the floor, then place a second sheet on top. Sketch the shape of a large animal or character on one side, then cut through both thicknesses to make two like shapes. Let the children paint and decorate both sides with paint, chalk, markers, crayons, or collage materials. Staple the edges together $3/4$ of the way around. Ask the children to tear up small strips of newspaper and stuff them inside the shape. Staple the opening closed. Hang on a wall or from the ceiling.

Variations:

Make giant shapes that relate to a theme or interest of the children.

Let each child make his or her own giant shape. It could be a snowman, butterfly, dinosaur, etc. Provide paints, fabric scraps, markers, wallpaper, and other collage materials to decorate it with.

Cut large objects out of foam board and let the children decorate them with markers and collage materials. Hang from walls, doors, or the ceiling.

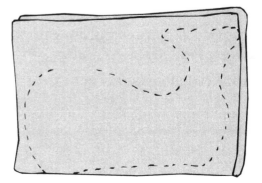

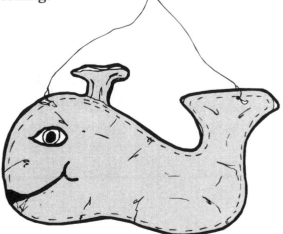

Classroom Quilts

Social skills will flourish as children work together to create a quilt for their classroom. Quilts also reflect community effort and the beauty that evolves as individuals work together.

Materials:

- fabric crayons
- paper, iron
- squares of inexpensive white cloth or muslin

Directions:

Have the children draw designs on a piece of paper with the fabric crayons. (Remind them to press hard and make their designs as colorful as possible.) Place the picture on the fabric face down; iron with a medium iron, pressing hard until the color transfers. Sew or tape the squares together. Add backing if you desire.

Hint:

If you write on the paper, you must do so backwards so that when it is ironed it will be correct.

Burlap Stitchery

Materials:

- squares of burlap
- plastic needles
- yarn, scissors

Directions:

Let the children sew original designs on a square of burlap with yarn. Sew sections together or use cloth tape to hold them in place.

All of Us

Materials:

- paper cut in 8" squares
- multicultural markers and crayons
- hole punch
- yarn

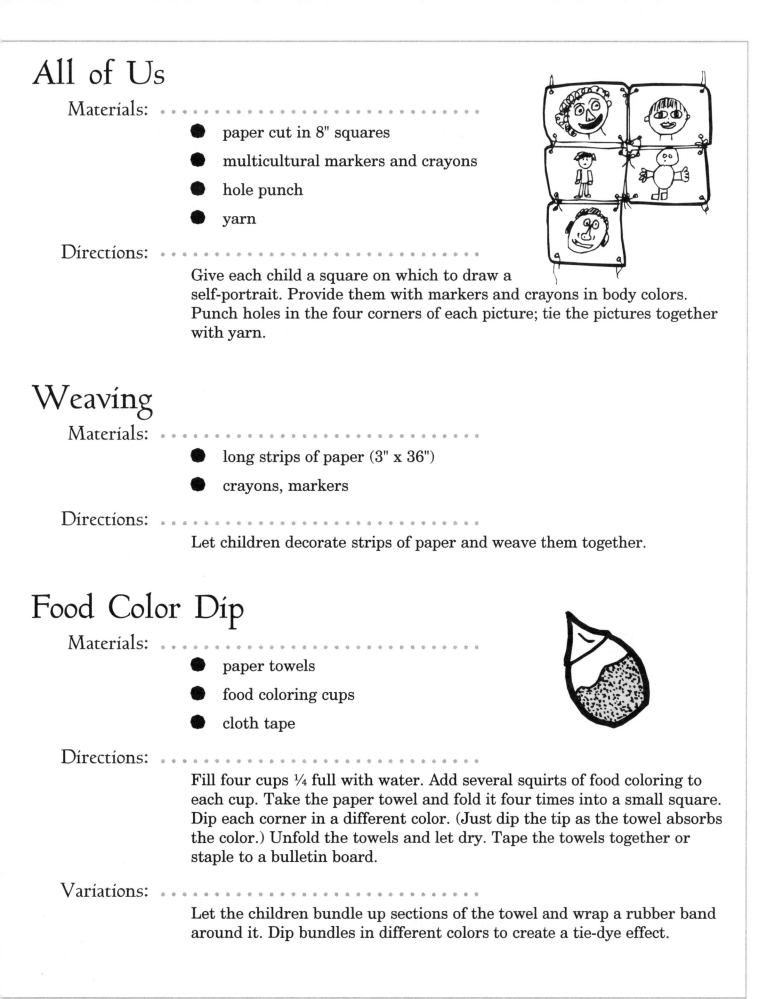

Directions:

Give each child a square on which to draw a self-portrait. Provide them with markers and crayons in body colors. Punch holes in the four corners of each picture; tie the pictures together with yarn.

Weaving

Materials:

- long strips of paper (3" x 36")
- crayons, markers

Directions:

Let children decorate strips of paper and weave them together.

Food Color Dip

Materials:

- paper towels
- food coloring cups
- cloth tape

Directions:

Fill four cups ¼ full with water. Add several squirts of food coloring to each cup. Take the paper towel and fold it four times into a small square. Dip each corner in a different color. (Just dip the tip as the towel absorbs the color.) Unfold the towels and let dry. Tape the towels together or staple to a bulletin board.

Variations:

Let the children bundle up sections of the towel and wrap a rubber band around it. Dip bundles in different colors to create a tie-dye effect.

Family Designs

Materials:

- squares of white fabric or muslin

Directions:

Send home a square with each child; have the children decorate their squares with their parents. Sew the squares together.

Variations:

Decorate pieces of white poster board cut in 2" squares, and tape to a wall to create a quilt.

Crazy Quilt

Materials:

- pictures, paintings, printing, collages, and other art
- projects children have left at school without their names
- poster board
- glue

Directions:

Cut the projects into geometric shapes and arrange on the poster board. Glue in place. Add a border to give it a finished look.

Puzzle

Materials:

- large piece of corrugated cardboard or poster board
- scissors
- markers, crayons

Directions:

Cut the cardboard into puzzle pieces. Make enough so each child in your class can have a piece of the puzzle to decorate with markers or crayons. Glue or tape together.

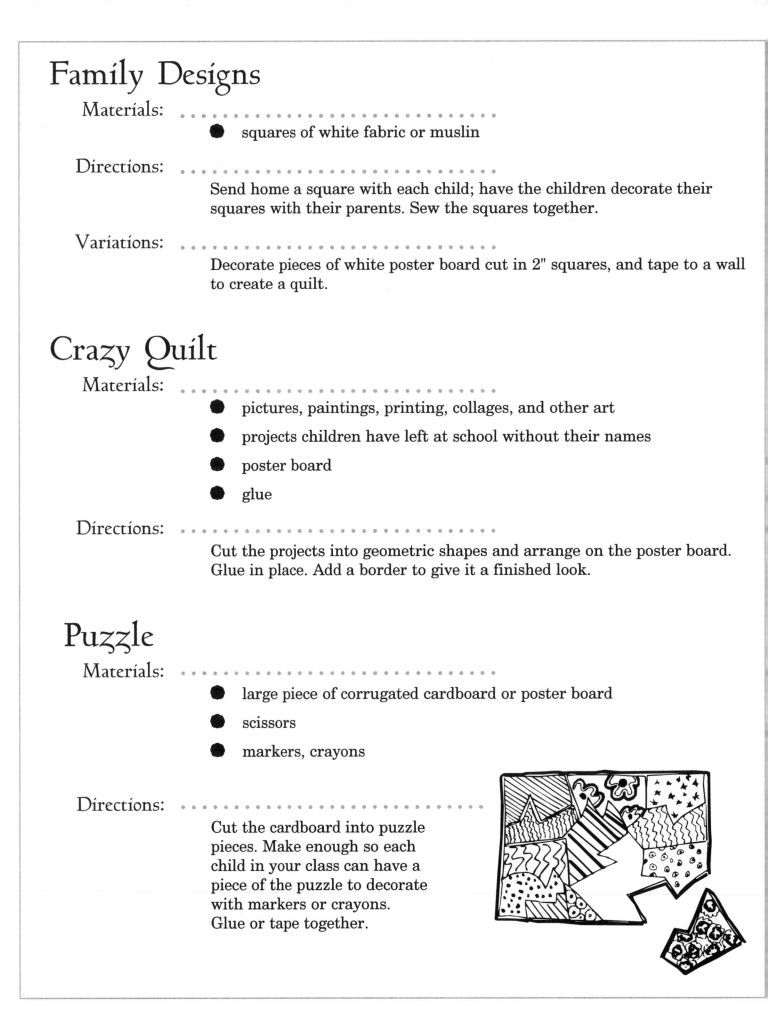

"Me" Pictures

Children love themselves and will enjoy drawing their pictures with these ideas.

Look At Me

Materials:

- mirror
- paper
- body color crayons, markers, and paints

Directions:

Hang a mirror by the art easel so the children can look at themselves as they draw their portraits.

Happy Faces

Materials:

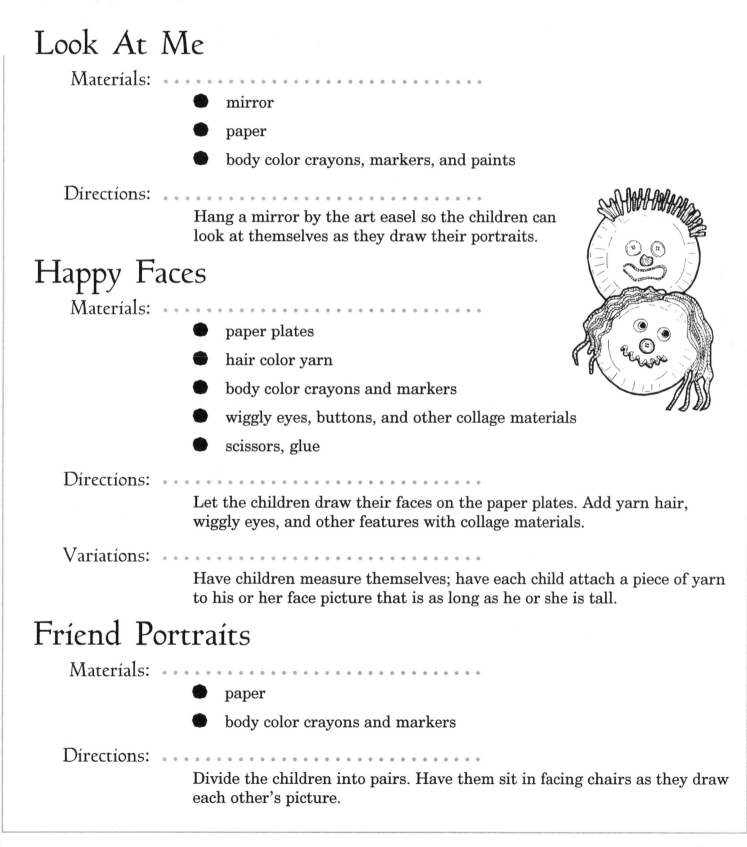

- paper plates
- hair color yarn
- body color crayons and markers
- wiggly eyes, buttons, and other collage materials
- scissors, glue

Directions:

Let the children draw their faces on the paper plates. Add yarn hair, wiggly eyes, and other features with collage materials.

Variations:

Have children measure themselves; have each child attach a piece of yarn to his or her face picture that is as long as he or she is tall.

Friend Portraits

Materials:

- paper
- body color crayons and markers

Directions:

Divide the children into pairs. Have them sit in facing chairs as they draw each other's picture.

When I Grow Up

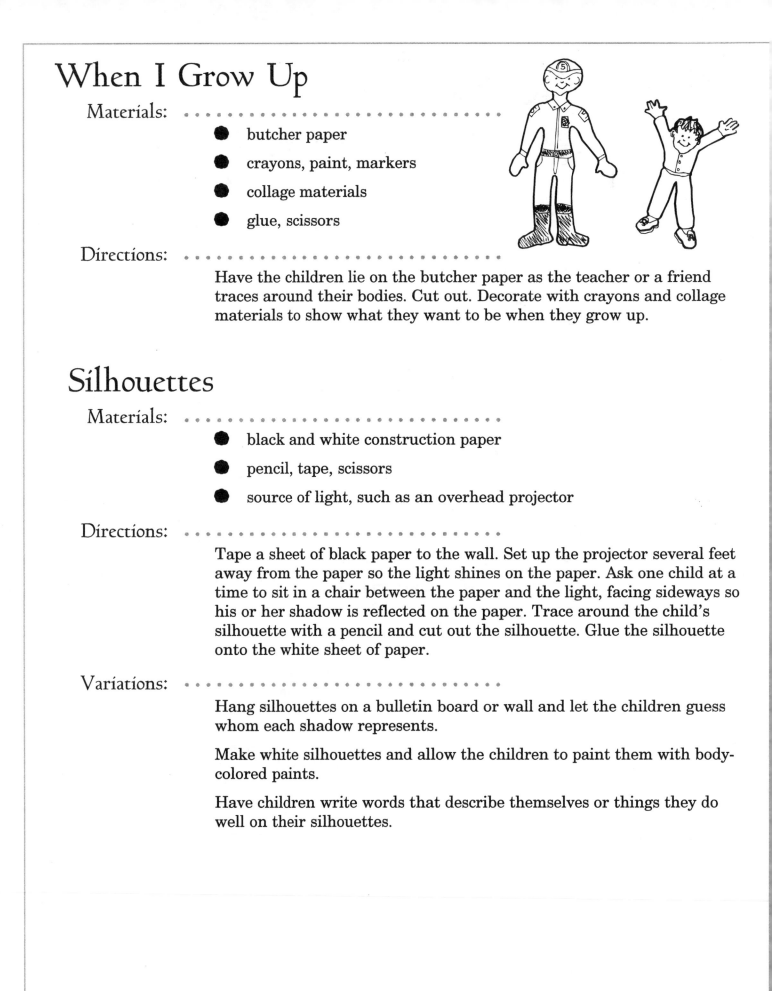

Materials: . . . .

- butcher paper
- crayons, paint, markers
- collage materials
- glue, scissors

Directions: . . . .

Have the children lie on the butcher paper as the teacher or a friend traces around their bodies. Cut out. Decorate with crayons and collage materials to show what they want to be when they grow up.

Silhouettes

Materials: . . . .

- black and white construction paper
- pencil, tape, scissors
- source of light, such as an overhead projector

Directions: . . . .

Tape a sheet of black paper to the wall. Set up the projector several feet away from the paper so the light shines on the paper. Ask one child at a time to sit in a chair between the paper and the light, facing sideways so his or her shadow is reflected on the paper. Trace around the child's silhouette with a pencil and cut out the silhouette. Glue the silhouette onto the white sheet of paper.

Variations: . . . .

Hang silhouettes on a bulletin board or wall and let the children guess whom each shadow represents.

Make white silhouettes and allow the children to paint them with body-colored paints.

Have children write words that describe themselves or things they do well on their silhouettes.

Artistic Impressions

Enhance aesthetic appreciation and expose children to famous artists with this idea.

Materials:

- old art books (available at used book stores, college book stores, garages sales, etc.)
- bulletin board or poster board
- glue, scissors
- construction paper

Directions:

Choose an artist and cut out several of his or her pictures. Mount the pictures attractively on construction paper and arrange them on a bulletin board with the artist's name. Introduce the children to the "artist of the month" by giving a little biographical information about the artist. Tell the children the titles of the pictures and discuss the materials used to create them. Encourage children's comments about how the pictures make them feel. Introduce a new artist to the children each month.

Variations:

Art calendars and postcards also work well for this project.

Make a "Big Book of Artists" by cutting pieces of poster board in half. Put pictures by artists you have introduced to the children on the poster board; attach the pieces together with book rings. Look through the book with the children to see if they can identify different artists' work.

Invite an artist to visit your classroom, or take the children on a field trip to an art museum.

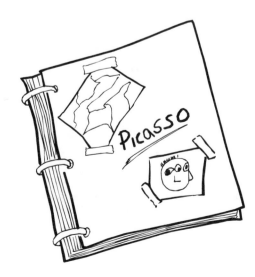

The Great Frame-Up

Take the time to display children's work with some of these simple frames.

Bits and Pieces

Materials: . . . .

- mat board or poster board
- utility knife
- children's artwork
- tape

Directions: . . . .

Cut various geometric or abstract shapes out of the poster board with the utility knife. Tape a different piece of art behind each opening. (Label with the children's names and the process used.)

Variations: . . . .

Add a border or mount on contrasting poster board.

Mat It

Materials: . . . .

- black construction paper
- scissors
- rubber cement

Directions: . . . .

Take black construction paper the size of the art project and cut out an oval or rectangle from the center. Glue this over the picture and label with the child's name and description of how the artwork was made.

Variations: . . . .

Ask art or frame shops to save their mat scraps for you.

Paper Frames

Materials:
- construction paper
- rubber cement

Directions:

Cut the construction paper so it is 2" to 4" longer and wider than the project to be framed. Glue the project to the middle of the construction paper, then crease in all the edges of the construction paper so they stand up and make a shadow-box frame.

Variations:

Use shirt boxes or gift boxes as frames for art.

Glue art to cardboard, then glue popsicle sticks around the edges to create a border.

Fun Frames

Materials:
- poster board or cardboard
- scissors
- jigsaw puzzle pieces
- glue

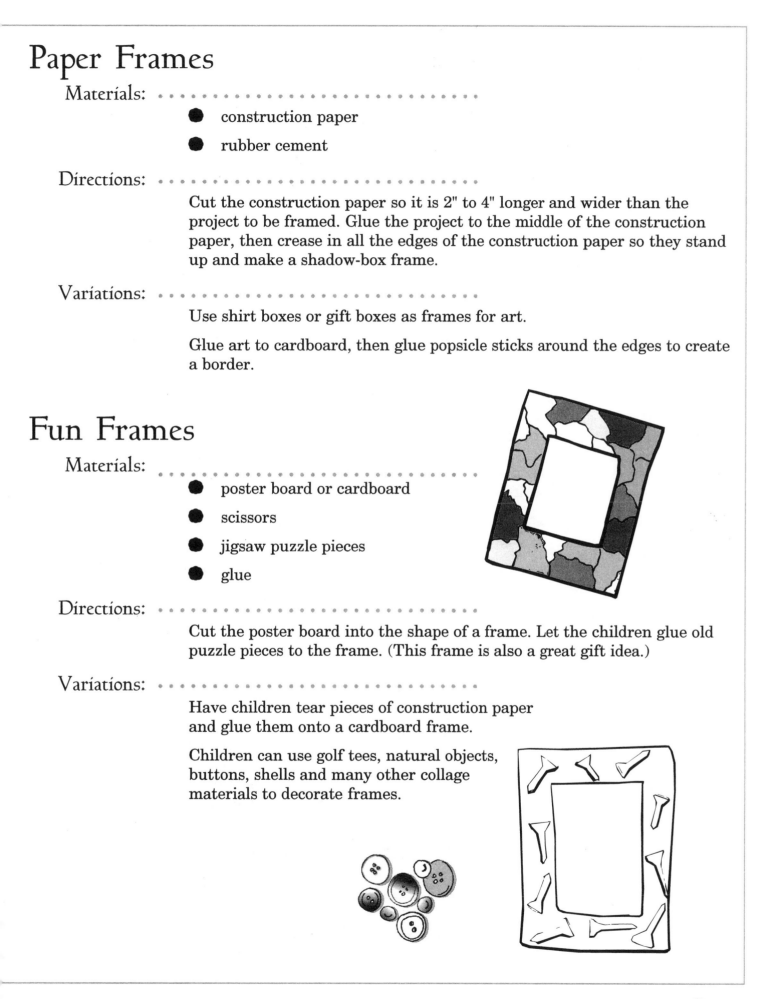

Directions:

Cut the poster board into the shape of a frame. Let the children glue old puzzle pieces to the frame. (This frame is also a great gift idea.)

Variations:

Have children tear pieces of construction paper and glue them onto a cardboard frame.

Children can use golf tees, natural objects, buttons, shells and many other collage materials to decorate frames.

Peek-A-Boo

Children will be surprised by peek-a-boo and hidden pictures.

Materials:

- poster board
- fabric scraps
- tape, glue
- colorful pictures

Directions:

Glue four or five pictures onto the poster board. (Cut out pictures of things your children would enjoy.) Cut a piece of fabric to cover each picture. Tape the fabric to the top of each picture. Hang the peek-a-boo poster on the back of a shelf or door for children to lift and see the pictures.

Variations:

Play a guessing game to see if the children can remember where a certain picture is hidden.

Tape a towel or blanket over a small mirror so children can play peek-a-boo and see themselves.

Place different textures for the children to feel under the peek-a-boos.

Make peek-a-boo books. Glue pictures on construction paper. Cut flaps out of wallpaper and tape them over the pictures. Put several pages together to make a book.

Learning Centers = Child-Centered Classrooms

Centers are the most natural way to organize a classroom to enable children to become active learners.

Centers give children opportunities to make choices, explore at their own level, engage in hands-on discovery, solve problems, work with friends, use language, and be creative. Centers also allow children to move, involve a greater use of the senses, and are an effective way to use classroom materials, time, and space. Howard Gardner, author of *Multiple Intelligences*, recommends that classrooms be set up like "discovery museums." Clearly, learning centers support this theory and the child's total development by encouraging many different interests and talents. Above all, learning centers are fun and capitalize on *play*, which is the most meaningful way for children to learn.

Remember—with learning centers, the teacher's role is that of a facilitator. Provide children with challenges, opportunities to learn, and open-ended materials, then trust them to construct their own knowledge in their own unique ways.

Research suggests that children need large blocks of time — 45 minutes minimum — to explore learning activities and really get involved in them. Research further emphasizes the importance of carefully selecting materials and equipment that meet the developmental needs and interests of the children. With too many toys and props, children focus on the objects rather than interacting with each other. On the other hand, if there are too few materials, children will fight over toys and become aggressive.

Centers that should be available in your classroom include:

blocks	writing
dramatic play	sensory play
art	music
manipulatives	large motor
science	construction
math (computers)	library

Not all of these centers have to be set up in your classroom at the same time. For example, construction and sensory play could be rotated. Other centers can easily be combined, such as science and math, and writing and manipulatives. The library center could be combined with the quiet place (see page 56).

Consider these guidelines in arranging your classroom to create interest areas that will enhance play, social interaction, independence, and learning:*

- Arrange centers according to the noise and activity level. For example, quieter centers such as the library, manipulatives, and science should be grouped together, while blocks, dramatic play, and art should be in another area.

- Partition the classroom with shelves, bookcases, play units, and dividers to create smaller spaces. With large open areas, children are more likely to run, and to have difficulty concentrating.

- Provide children with at least four activities to choose from in each center. Arrange the toys so the children can easily take them out and put them back in place.

- Avoid clutter in centers by rotating materials.

- Art, sensory play, and eating areas should be on washable flooring. Carpeting in blocks, dramatic play, and the library adds warmth and will keep the noise down.

- Think about the natural flow and traffic patterns in the classroom. Art and sensory play should be near the sink, cubbies near the door, science by a window, music close to an electrical outlet, etc.

- Draw a floor plan of your classroom and cut out scaled shapes to represent furniture and equipment. Try different arrangements until you get optimal use of your space.

- Get down on your knees to get a "child's-eye view" of the classroom. Stand up for a "teacher's-eye view" to make sure you can supervise the children at all times.

* The National Association for the Education of Young Children (NAEYC) provides excellent criteria for setting up positive classroom environments for children in their accreditation materials. Call 800-424-2460 for additional information.

Center Management

There are many different ways to manage learning centers, and the one that is best is the one that works for you. The ages and abilities of your children, as well as your goals and philosophy, will influence your choice of strategies.

Choice Board ....

Make a poster board with illustrations of the different centers in your classroom. (Use real photographs or pictures from school supply catalogs for this.) Make dots to represent the number of children who can play in each center along the side as shown. Write each child's name on a clothespin. At center time, each child may put his clothespin on the center where he would like to play. When the child wants to change centers, he needs to get his clothespin and select another area that has an empty space.

Graphs ....

Put up a graph each week in the centers with all the children's names. Have children color in their names on the graph when they go to each center.

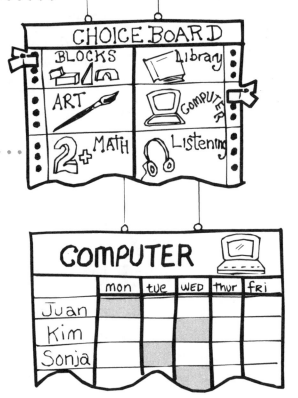

Contracts ....

Give each child a contract (these can be done daily or weekly) with the different centers listed. As children complete activities, they can color in the appropriate section on their contract.

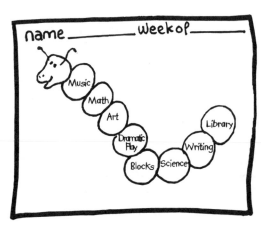

Center Necklace

Choose a different color for each center in your classroom. For example, "blocks" could be brown, "library" purple, "manipulatives" red, etc. Cover coffee cans with construction paper the color of each center and put them in the appropriate areas. Next, color clothespins with markers to match the centers. (You will need one of each color for every child.) Make a "center necklace" for each child with a 30" piece of ribbon or string. Have each child decorate a 3" cardboard circle with her name, punch a hole in it, and string it on her necklace. On Monday, pass out the clothespins for each center and have the children hang them on their necklaces. Explain the different activities they can do at the centers that week. As children go to different centers during the week, they take their clothespins of that color and put them in the can of the corresponding color. (Have the children store their necklaces in their cubbies and only wear them at center time.) If children finish all of their centers by Friday, they get to do a special activity. This method encourages children to take responsibility for their own learning and manage their time.

Individual Conferences

Ask children individually where they would like to play and what they plan to do there. Use a puppet, play telephone, microphone, or other prop to do this. Follow up after center time by asking the children what they did or by having them draw pictures in their journals.

Sign Off

Hang a list of children's names by each center and ask them to cross their names off after they have played there. They could also sign their names to a sheet of paper on a clipboard as they go to different centers.

Card Punch

Print the numerals from 1 to 4 on index cards (or use numerals to include the number of centers in your classroom). Give each child a card and ask him to write his name on it. Number the different centers in the classroom; as children have completed a task or finished playing in that area, the teacher can punch a hole in their cards next to the corresponding numeral. (Cards can be used for a week by adding more centers and numerals on index cards.)

Bracelets, Aprons, Hats or Clothespins

Use colored bracelets, clothespins, hats, aprons, or other props children can wear as they play in a center. For example, children who want to play in blocks could wear a construction hat; children who want to play in the art area could put on an apron; children who want to play with a computer could wear a bracelet. (Have the same number of props as the number of children you want in the area at one time.)

Picture Cards

Cut out pictures representative of the different centers in your classroom from school supply catalogs. (Cut out the same number of pictures for each area as children who can play in that area.) Glue the pictures to poster-board cards cut in 4" squares. At center time, shuffle up the cards and have each child draw one. Each child then goes to the center on his card.

Observation . . . .

Observe children, then guide them to areas where they can enhance skills.
Pair children with different abilities to play games or work on tasks so
they can learn from each other.

Look and See . . . .

Write each child's name down the left side of a poster board. Attach three
small adhesive hooks beside each child's name. Cut out 3" circles and
punch a hole in the top of each one. Write the names of different centers
in the classroom on the circles. Each day put three different centers beside
each child's name for her to complete that day. Children do the assigned
centers in sequence, then are given free choice.

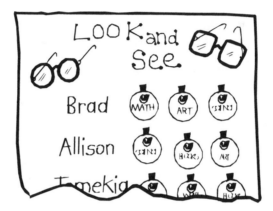

Hints:

Children need to work for a minimum of 45 minutes to an hour every day
in learning centers in order to engage in elaborate and meaningful play.

When limiting the number of children who can play in a center at a given
time, it is best to use even numbers, such as two or four.

Learning Centers Book

Children will enjoy making and reading this learning centers book. It is also an effective way to communicate with parents about developmentally appropriate practices and the value of learning through play.

Materials:

- construction paper cut into 9" x 12" pieces
- photographs of the children playing in different learning centers
- scissors, glue, hole punch
- 2 book rings
- markers, crayons

Directions:

Make a cover for the book called "Learning Is Fun." On each page, glue a photograph of a learning center and write a description similar to those on the following page. Hole-punch the pages and put them together with book rings. Read the book to the children, then let them "read" it to each other by telling about the pictures. Allow one child to take home the book each day to share with his family.

Variations:

Use pictures of different learning centers from school supply catalogs if you don't have photographs.

Let the children draw pictures of themselves playing in the different centers, then have them dictate what they do in each center to use as the text for the book.

Ask each child to draw a picture about what she likes best at school. Put the pages together in a book called "School Is Fun."

Learning Center Fun

Blocks

In the block center I'm developing math concepts and motor skills. I'm also learning how to share and work with my friends. I may use these skills as an architect or builder when I grow up.

Library

In the library I'm learning to love books and I'm practicing my reading skills.

Art

The art center gives me the opportunity to develop my creativity and express myself. As I experiment and have fun, I'm also developing social skills and small muscles.

Dramatic Play

When I pretend and play dress-up, I'm learning how to be a mommy, daddy, doctor, teacher, or police officer. Dramatic play also fosters my language and social skills.

Science

I can observe, experiment, predict, and discover new things in the science area. These are the same things real scientists do.

Math

The math center develops my problem-solving skills and gives me hands-on experiences in counting, comparing, patterning, and measuring. I may use these skills as an accountant or computer specialist when I grow up.

Music

As I play instruments and sing, I'm expressing myself and developing listening and language skills. Music just makes me feel good!

Writing

The writing center has lots of interesting materials so I can learn how to write stories, letters, books, and more. Maybe I'll be an author when I grow up.

Manipulatives

When I play with puzzles and manipulative materials, I'm developing eye-hand coordination and learning to complete tasks.

Outdoors

Out on the playground, I'm releasing energy and developing strength, coordination, and a strong, healthy body. I love to play outside with my friends at school.

I am working, playing and discovering in my own way in learning centers each day!

Reproducible page

Around the Room with

A multicultural curriculum is one that represents people of all ethnic groups, ages, sexes, and abilities in meaningful ways. These are some exciting ideas for implementing the anti-bias curriculum in learning centers.

Dramatic Play
Use food containers and utensils for different ethnic foods; multiethnic dolls; clothes, shoes, hats, and jewelry from a variety of cultures; full-length mirrors.

Library
Include folk tales from different cultures; books representative of all our society; printed materials in different languages.

Manipulatives
Provide nonsexist puzzles; graduated stacking dolls from another culture; coins and beads from other countries.

Art
Offer children crayons, markers, paint, and clay in various body colors; art media of other cultures (i.e. cloth, rice paper); pictures of art from different areas of the world.

Cooking
Let children prepare ethnic foods; include ethnic meals on the monthly menu.

Multicultural Ideas

Music

Play tapes and songs from around the world; use ethnic instruments.

Blocks

Show pictures of different kinds of homes (mobile homes, apartments, single-family dwellings; rural, sub-urban, urban; houses from other countries); multiethnic figures; different types of transportations; a variety of building materials, such as straw, sticks, canvas.

Sensory

Give children animals from different habitats (arctic, rainforest, desert, forest) to play with in sand and water.

Math

Make graphs that compare families; manipulatives from different cultures; counting books in different languages.

Pictures

Display pictures of different families and ethnic groups; pictures that reflect diversity; men and women in different roles; children with varying abilities; pictures of children in the room and their families.

Block Center

Blocks help children develop concepts of number, size, shape, space, and weight. They also encourage imagination, language, social skills, self-confidence, and motor skills. Further, blocks give children a great deal of personal satisfaction and pleasure.

Materials:

unit blocks — various shapes
  and sizes
shelf
carpeted floor
Legos
cardboard boxes
alphabet blocks
wooden dollhouse and furniture
wooden barn and animals
plastic dinosaurs or zoo animals
toy train set, boats, airplanes
small dolls or action figures
plastic bins or boxes for
  accessories
foam blocks
wooden cars and trucks
toy street signs

Lincoln Logs
Bristle Blocks
hollow blocks
construction hats
carpenter's apron
blueprints
paper, pencils
maps
tile or carpet samples

Teacher Tips:

Place blocks on a carpeted area away from quiet areas, such as the library or writing center.

Enclose the block area on three sides with cabinets or shelves.

Provide enough space in the block center so several children can move around and build on the floor.

Limit the number of children who can play in the block area at one time.

Trace around the shapes of different unit blocks on dark construction paper and cut them out. Tape these shapes to shelves or cover with clear contact paper to help children with clean-up time.

Group like props in tubs, pails, or baskets and label with the words and pictures.

Use a large leaf basket to store blocks and have the children put all the blocks in it when they pick up.

Assign one child each day to be "block chairperson" and be responsible for cleaning up the block center.

If children have worked hard on a structure or are not finished, allow them to leave it with a sign that says, "Please do not disturb." You can also designate a shelf as the "block gallery" where children can save their creations, or take photographs of what the children build.

Post simple rules in the block area.

Build only as tall as you are.

Only knock down what you build.

Put the blocks away when you're finished.

Block Props

Idea Box ....

Make an idea box with pictures of different things children can build, such as a bridge, library, park, or machine.

Themes ....

Relate blocks to stories or themes. For example, children could build a castle for Cinderella, a space station, or a model of your community.

Street Signs ....

Cut out labels and logos from bags and advertisements. Tape these to craft sticks, then place the sticks in clay balls to make road signs. Children can also make road signs from construction paper and tape them onto sticks or toilet paper rolls.

Paper Logs ....

Roll up newspaper into tubes and tape them together to make log houses.

Roads ....

Use masking tape or colored cloth tape on the floor to make roads and highways.

Labels ....

Encourage the children to make homemade signs and labels, such as "hospital" or "airport," for their buildings and structures.

City Sites ....

Glue pictures of buildings, homes, or other sites in your community to shoe boxes; use with toy vehicles.

Pattern Cards ....

Make block pattern cards where children can practice making patterns and following directions.

Buildings ....

Cover shoe boxes, oatmeal canisters, or food boxes with newspaper or aluminum foil. Decorate with construction paper scraps to make doors and windows and use as buildings.

Houses

Make houses from paper lunch sacks. You will need two sacks. Fill one sack with crumpled newspaper. Turn the other sack upside down and decorate it with markers or crayons to look like a house or building. Insert the decorated sack over the stuffed sack so it will stand up.

Floor Map

Involve the children in designing a floor map by drawing with markers on a piece of foam board. (Floor maps can also be made by gluing felt scraps on a large piece of felt fabric.)

People Props

Tape photographs of the children or pictures they have drawn to toilet paper rolls and use as props in the block center.

Scale

Add a balance scale to the block area so children can weigh blocks and discuss "heavy" and "light."

Measurement

Have the children use blocks to measure different objects in the classroom. For example, challenge them to find out how many blocks tall a table is, how many blocks long the room is, or how many blocks tall different friends are.

Homemade Props

Involve the children in making their own props, such as puppets, paper hats, clay animals, and scenery, for the block center.

Hide and Go Seek

Hide unit blocks of different geometric shapes (square, triangle, rectangle, and cylinder) around the classroom. Give children a specific shape to find and bring back to you.

Box Blocks

Stuff empty diaper boxes, cereal boxes, detergent boxes, or cardboard milk cartons with crumpled newspaper. Cover with contact paper to make blocks.

Dramatic Play Center

In the dramatic play area children have the opportunity to role-play real-life situations, release emotions, practice language, develop social skills, and express themselves creatively.

Materials:

kitchen equipment (stove, refrigerator, sink, microwave)
pots, pans, dishes, ethnic cooking utensils
dress-up clothes (children's, men's, ladies')
night clothes (robes, gowns, slippers, pajamas)
pocketbooks, hats, clip-on ties
shoes (boots, sports shoes, children's, adult's, etc.)
full-length mirror
table and chairs
dolls and doll clothes (multiethnic dolls of both sexes)
stuffed animals
puppets
doll bed, blankets, pillows
baby carriage
ironing board and iron
empty food boxes and containers

telephones
old jewelry, jewelry box
broom, mop, carpet sweeper
books and magazines
paper, pencils, grocery lists
tablecloth, plastic flowers for the table
old camera
suitcase, briefcase, billfold, keys
costumes
vests

Teacher Tips:

Place the dramatic play center in a corner or define it with shelves so it is cozy.

Limit the number of children who can play in the center at a particular time.

Provide enough props to interest the children, but rotate materials so the center doesn't become cluttered and overwhelm them.

Use a clothes rack, pegboard, or plastic hooks with adhesive backs for hanging bags and clothes.

Laundry baskets can also be used for storing clothes and hats.

Cut out shapes of dishes and pans from contact paper and tape them on shelves to help children with clean-up time.

Knot bags or purses with long handles so children won't choke themselves. Cut off old clothes if they are too long so the children won't trip.

Housekeeping Props

Decorations ....

Make the dramatic play center homey with a rug, pictures, and curtains on the window.

Windows ....

Add a window by attaching a mirror or landscape picture to a wall. Tape on construction paper strips to look like a window frame, then add fabric or wallpaper cut like a curtain.

Washer and Dryer ....

Cut a circle out of the front of a corrugated cardboard box. Cut a door around it and add a pipe cleaner handle. Draw knobs, dials, and details on it to make it look like a washer or dryer.

Pantyhose Hair ....

Take an old pair of pantyhose and cut off the feet. Cut each leg into three strips and braid. Tie off the ends of each braid with a ribbon, then wear on the head like a wig.

Food ....

Glue pictures of food in pie pans or frozen dinner trays. You can also glue labels from cans of food to toilet paper rolls to make canned goods.

Placemats ....

Cut old plastic placemats in half for the dramatic play center. To make napkins, cut 12" squares from fabric. Napkin rings can be made by cutting 1" rings off of cardboard rollers and coloring them with markers.

Character Headbands ....

Cut animal ears out of felt and glue them onto plastic headbands. Make pink pig ears, black cat ears, floppy brown ears for a dog, etc.

Make-Up ....

Take old make-up (blush, eye shadow, powder) and pop out the contents with a knife. Cut colored felt and glue in place of the make-up. Store in an old make-up case with applicators and brushes. Empty a nail polish bottle. Clean the brush with remover and allow the remainder of the polish to evaporate. Fill with water so children can "paint" their nails.

Earrings ·

String beads on thin ribbon cut 7" long. Tie ends to make loops that children can hang on their ears.

Baby Bed ·

Use an old infant carrier or car seat as a baby bed in the housekeeping area. Children will also enjoy playing with old diaper bags, blankets, toys, bottles, clothes, and other baby accessories.

Pets ·

Add stuffed animal dogs and cats, pet bowls, dried dog biscuits, etc.

Phones ·

Recycle broken phones in the dramatic play area. (Wall phones are especially fun.) Make a cellular phone by covering a small box with black paper or aluminum foil. Write numerals on the phone with a marker and add a pipe cleaner for an antenna.

Babies ·

Cut a piece of flannel in a 20" to 30" square. Make a ball of polyester filling and place it in the middle of the square (back side). Wrap a rubber band around the filling to make a head. Tie ribbons around two ends to make arms. Decorate a face with fabric pens, or sew on button eyes and features. Add yarn hair if you wish.

Prop Boxes

Vary the dramatic play area with prop boxes that relate to different units of study, reflect children's interests, or extend a shared experience. All you need is a box or plastic tub for storage and some of the materials below. (A note to parents about an upcoming theme is a great way to get items for prop boxes.) These boxes can also be shared by different classrooms in the school.

Grocery Store ·

Empty food boxes and cans, grocery sacks, grocery cart or wagon, shelves, cash register, play money, cardboard boxes, paper and pencils, dress-up clothes, purses, billfolds (Set up a fruit stand, bakery, etc.)

Post Office ·

Envelopes, paper, pencils and pens, rubber stamps, stamp pad, stickers, partitioned box, cash register, play money, bag or sack for carrying mail, old hat, wagon for mail truck

Pet Shop ·

Stuffed animals, puppets, cardboard boxes for cages, plastic bowls, brush, towel, grooming supplies, cash register, pet toys

Restaurant ·

Paper plates, napkins, plastic cups, silverware, tray, notepad, pencils, apron, chef's hat, menus, cash register, play food, food pictures glued onto paper plates, telephone, carry-out food containers (Change it to be a pizza parlor, ice cream shop, or school cafeteria.)

Flower Shop ·

Plastic pots, artificial flowers, gloves, seed catalogs, baskets, watering can, play garden tools, phone, notepad, cash register

Doctor's Office/ Hospital ·

Stethoscope, tongue depressors, cotton, Band-Aids, eye chart, scale, empty medicine bottles, dolls, notepad and pencils, nurse's cap, wagon for ambulance, phone, scrub suit and mask

**Hat Shop/
Shoe Store** . . . .

Old shoes (men's, women's, babies',
childrens', etc.), hats (make in art),
purses, accessories, socks, mirror,
cash register, play money, hat rack,
shoe shine kit

Travel Agency . . . .

Travel posters, brochures, pamphlets, books on other countries, tickets,
desk, chairs, phone, calendar, notepad and pencils, souvenirs from other
countries, dress-up clothes

**Construction
Site** . . . .

Blueprints, hammer, nails, wood scraps, tape measure, paintbrushes, hard
hat, lunch box, safety glasses, carpenter's apron, gloves, toy trucks,
blocks, cardboard boxes, portable phone

Theater . . . .

Tickets, cash register, chairs, empty food boxes and cups for refreshments,
dress-up clothes, puppets, puppet theater, old costumes, mirror, jewelry,
hats, glasses, masks

Camp Site . . . .

Sleeping bag, backpack, canteen, stones and sticks for fire, blanket to
make a tent, play fishing pole

**Airport/Train
Station** . . . .

Phone, tickets, cash register, play money, paper and pencils, travel brochures, suitcase, dress-up clothes, chairs, food trays and paper goods,
cardboard boxes to make a train

Office . . . .

Typewriter, cash register, calculator, paper, pencils, envelopes,
phone, calendar, dress-up clothes
(adapt to make a bank, newspaper
office, etc.)

Fire or Police
Station
Paper badges, whistle, helmet or hat, phone, stamp pad, flashlight, paper and pencils, riding toys, ticket book, map, piece of hose, boots, air tank made from empty plastic liter bottles

School
Desk for teacher, bell, calendar, paper, crayons, pencils, books, chairs, dress-up clothes, eyeglass frames, chalkboard, flag, clock

Photo Studio
Old camera, film canisters, pictures, photo album, video camera (made from a cereal box and paper towel roll), phone, appointment book, paper and pencils

Filling Station
Old hose, cash register, credit cards (cut up Styrofoam trays), cars and trucks, phone, empty food packages, towel, empty spray bottle, riding toys

Party
Invitations, party plates, cups, napkins, hats, favors, goodie bags, wrapping paper, tape, ribbon, empty boxes, greeting cards

Variations:
An art shop, circus, boat, rocketship, costume shop, wedding, sports store, toy shop, library, music store, and TV station are other enjoyable subjects for prop boxes.

Art Center

By setting up an open art center in your classroom, children will have the opportunity to plan and create in their own unique ways. They will be able to make choices, experiment, solve problems, and be truly creative. Provide children with a wide variety of materials that they can get out and clean up independently. (Vary the number of materials to fit the age and abilities of the children.)

Materials:

shelves
easel
tables and chairs
drying rack
paints
body-colored paints, crayons, markers
brushes
hole punch
paper (scrap, construction, cardboard)
scissors
crayons
paper sacks
paper cups
newspaper
glue, glue sticks
paper plates
tissue paper
material scraps
buttons
stapler

junk scraps (toilet paper rolls, egg cartons)
tape
cotton
magazines, catalogs
yarn
fingerpaint
wallpaper book
chalk
brads
paper clips
clay
play dough
popsicle sticks
foil
watercolors
rubber cement
pipe cleaners
colored pencils
natural objects (leaves, sticks, rocks)
prints or postcards of famous artwork

Teacher Tips:

Place the art center near a sink on a washable floor. It should also be out of the flow of traffic.

Have sponges, paper towels, and a trash can handy so the children can clean up their own messes.

Use old adult shirts for smocks.

Cover the table and floor with newspaper for easy clean-up of messy projects.

Put out a few materials at a time for younger children. (They are overwhelmed if they have too many choices.)

Take time to show the children how to use and care for different materials. For example, how to use "just one dot of glue" or how to "put the paintbrush back in the same color."

Artful Hints

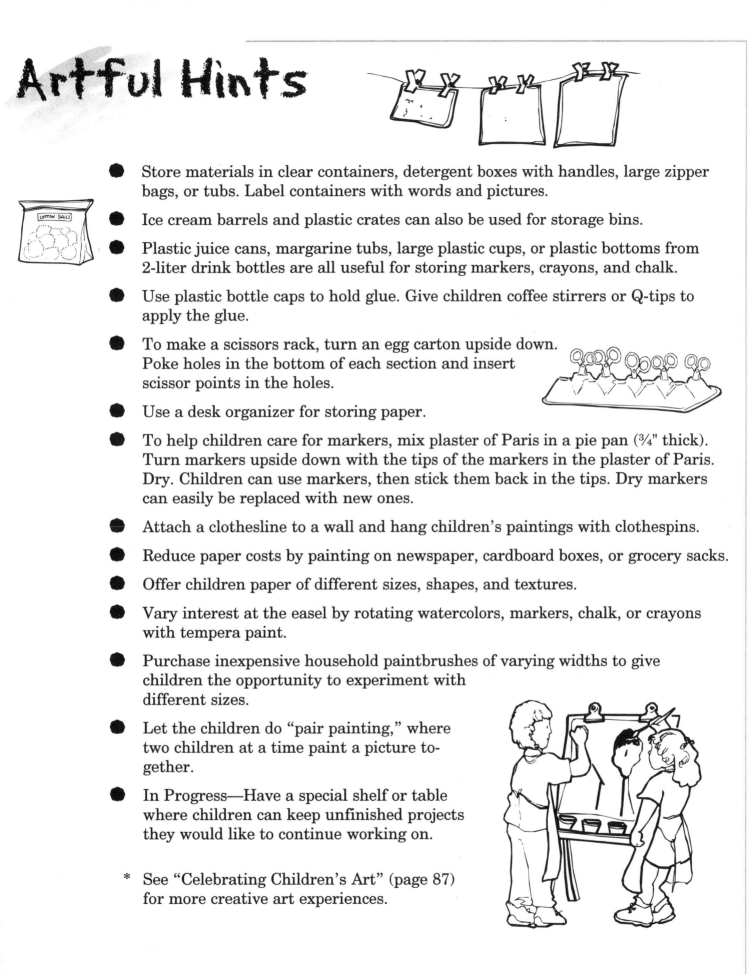

- Store materials in clear containers, detergent boxes with handles, large zipper bags, or tubs. Label containers with words and pictures.

- Ice cream barrels and plastic crates can also be used for storage bins.

- Plastic juice cans, margarine tubs, large plastic cups, or plastic bottoms from 2-liter drink bottles are all useful for storing markers, crayons, and chalk.

- Use plastic bottle caps to hold glue. Give children coffee stirrers or Q-tips to apply the glue.

- To make a scissors rack, turn an egg carton upside down. Poke holes in the bottom of each section and insert scissor points in the holes.

- Use a desk organizer for storing paper.

- To help children care for markers, mix plaster of Paris in a pie pan (¾" thick). Turn markers upside down with the tips of the markers in the plaster of Paris. Dry. Children can use markers, then stick them back in the tips. Dry markers can easily be replaced with new ones.

- Attach a clothesline to a wall and hang children's paintings with clothespins.

- Reduce paper costs by painting on newspaper, cardboard boxes, or grocery sacks.

- Offer children paper of different sizes, shapes, and textures.

- Vary interest at the easel by rotating watercolors, markers, chalk, or crayons with tempera paint.

- Purchase inexpensive household paintbrushes of varying widths to give children the opportunity to experiment with different sizes.

- Let the children do "pair painting," where two children at a time paint a picture together.

- In Progress—Have a special shelf or table where children can keep unfinished projects they would like to continue working on.

  * See "Celebrating Children's Art" (page 87) for more creative art experiences.

Manipulatives

As children play with table toys they develop small muscles, eye-hand coordination, attention span, social skills, and language. They also build concepts about size, shape, color, and patterns.

Materials

table and chairs
puzzles
beads
sewing cards
pegboard
dressing toys
stacking toys
nuts and bolts
scissors
clay
pattern cards
snap toys
playing cards
shelves
puzzle rack
board games
lacing activities

Etch-a-Sketch
nesting toys
locks and keys
take-apart toys
hole punch
play dough and props
parquetry blocks
paper and pencils

Teacher Tips:

Store materials in clear containers, baskets, tubs, boxes, or plastic bags at the children's eye level. Recycled ice cream buckets, detergent boxes, or cut-down plastic milk jugs can also be used.

Use pictures from the boxes the toys come in to label the shelves.

Group like objects together.

Rotate manipulatives so the shelves don't look cluttered. Children should have from 10 to 15 activities to choose from at a time.

Discard manipulatives with missing pieces or broken parts. Clean plastic toys frequently.

Manipulative Activities

Puzzles . . . .

Make your own puzzles with cereal and food boxes. Cut off the front of the box and cut it into puzzle shapes. (Vary the number of puzzle pieces according to the ability of the children.)

Craft Stick Puzzles . . . .

Tape eight large craft sticks together. Turn them over and draw a picture with magic markers on the sticks. Remove the tape, mix up the sticks, and ask the children to put them back together.

Stencils . . . .

Cut shapes out of food boxes and plastic lids to make stencils and templates. Children will also enjoy tracing around puzzle pieces, cookie cutters, cans, and other common objects.

Floor Puzzle . . . .

Make a large floor puzzle from poster board or corrugated cardboard.

Match Ups . . . .

Collect plastic containers and lids from peanut butter, soft drink, syrup, and other foods. Children can match the containers with the lids, and screw the lids onto the containers.

Inserting . . . .

Cut a slit in the lid of a potato chip canister. Give the children poker chips and ask them to put them in the hole. Children can also insert pom poms in the mouth of a milk jug.

Sewing Cards . . . .

Punch holes in food boxes or paper plates, then give children shoelaces or cord so they can sew around them. Old plastic placemats can also be used to make lacing cards.

Pick Up . . . .

Give children chopsticks, tweezers, or tongs and challenge them to pick up different objects, such as small toys, cotton balls, rocks, or leaves.

Stringing . . . .

Let children string pasta with holes, cut-up straws, buttons, or cereal with holes on yarn or string to make a necklace. (Wrap a piece of tape around the end of the yarn so it is easier to thread the objects.)

Play Dough

RECIPE FOR HOMEMADE
PLAY DOUGH:

2 cups all purpose flour

1 cup salt

2 Tb. cream of tartar

2 Tb. vegetable oil

2 cups water

food coloring

Directions:

Mix all the ingredients together in a pan and stir until smooth. Cook over medium heat until the mixture forms a ball and sticks to the spoon. Cool and knead. Store in plastic bags or covered containers.

Add oil of mint or other extracts to play dough to give it a fragrance.

To make play dough that is body-colored, simply follow the directions above, omitting the food coloring. After the mixture has cooked, divide the dough into four balls. Add a different spice (such as cinnamon, chili powder, cocoa, curry, or paprika) to each ball and squeeze to mix. Give the children wiggly eyes and pipe cleaners to make people.

Have the children play with dough and clay on old placements. Add scissors, cookie cutters, play dishes, birthday candles, and other cooking props.

Flubber

Flubber feels good, gooey, and fun!

FLUBBER

2 cups white glue

1 1/2 cup water

food coloring

2 level tsp. Borax soap

1 cup hot water

Directions:

Combine the glue, 1½ cups water, and food coloring. In a large bowl dissolve the Borax in the hot water. Slowly stir the glue mixture into the Borax. It will coagulate and be difficult to mix. Pour off the excess water, then let it sit for several minutes. Drain off the remaining water. Store flubber covered in the refrigerator when it is not being used.

Goop

RECIPE FOR GOOP

Place 1 cup of cornstarch in a bowl. Slowly stir in enough water (1/2-3/4 cup) to make a thick liquid. Hold the goop in your hand, then let it run back into the bowl.

How is goop like a liquid? How is it like a solid?

Remind the children to always wash their hands before and after playing with play dough, flubber, or goop.

Science Center

In the science center children are able to explore, solve problems, make decisions, develop concepts about science and nature, improve language, interact socially, and develop sensory skills. Children's curiosity about the world and their interest in natural phenomena are also extended.

Materials:

- shelves, tables
- magnifying glass
- magnets
- plants
- prism
- animals and cage
- aquarium
- balance scale
- experiments
- science books, magazines
- pictures and posters
- thermometer
- flashlight
- color paddles
- feely box
- terrarium
- sensory activities
- models (dinosaurs, insects)
- mirror
- seeds, nuts, leaves, flowers, bird nests, feathers
- exhibits (nature collections of rocks, shells, bones, butterflies, etc.)
- field guide books
- clipboard, paper, pencils
- planting area to grow sprouts, flowers, herbs, etc.

Teacher Tips:

Arrange the science center in a quiet area of the classroom so individual or small groups of children can explore. (A window nearby is helpful for growing plants or for watching the world.)

Organize the materials in baskets, tubs, or on trays and rotate collections frequently to spark new interest.

Label the objects in the science area and add field guides, books, posters, and magazines so children can do research.

Encourage the children and parents to add to the science center with objects they find in their yard or on trips.

Place bird nests and other fragile specimens in zipper bags or clear deli containers so the children can investigate them with a magnifying glass.

Super Science Ideas

Color Paddles

Color paddles can be made with paper plates and red, yellow, and blue acetate (clear report folders or overhead projector sheets work well). Cut circles out of the acetate the size of the plates. Cut the centers out of six plates. Take the red acetate and staple it between two paper plates. Do the same for the blue and yellow. The children can hold up the plates and experiment with making the secondary colors.

Feely Socks

You will need six large plastic cups and six old socks for this sensory game. Stick a cup down into the toe of each sock. Place a common classroom object, such as a crayon, block, ball of clay, eraser, spoon, or toy car, into the cup in each sock. Draw a picture of each item on an index card. Have the children feel the object inside the socks and match up the pictures with the appropriate sock.

Sounds Like

Take ten empty film containers. Put rice in two of the containers, popcorn kernels in two, paper clips in two, salt in two, and pennies in two. Glue the tops onto the containers and mix them up. Let the children try to find the ones that sound alike.

Sniff and Tell

Put items with distinct smells (bubble gum, cocoa, peanut butter, cinnamon sticks, coffee grounds, baby powder) in the bottoms of different film containers. Glue on the lids, then poke several holes in the top. Children can smell each container and try to identify the odor. (To freshen smells, put a drop of water in the holes and shake.)

New Pennies

Mix a cup of vinegar with 2 Tb. of salt. Let the children take old pennies and stir them in this solution to make "shiny new pennies."

Volcano! . . . .

Fill a pie pan with sand. Put a bottle in the middle and build up around it with the sand. Pour ½ cup vinegar in the bottle and add several drops of red food coloring. Add 2 Tb. of baking soda to the vinegar and look out!

Mirror Magic . . . .

Cut small pictures from magazines or catalogs in half and glue one half of each picture onto a file folder. The children can take a small hand mirror and put it next to the picture to make the other half.

Research and Read . . . .

Collect leaves from different trees on the playground. Give the children a field guide book of trees and challenge them to identify the leaves by matching them up with pictures in the book. (Children can do similar activities with shell and rock collections.)

Hairy Plants . . . .

Draw a face on a plain paper cup. Fill the cup with dirt and sprinkle grass seed on top. Water and place in the sun. When the "hair" (grass) gets long, give it a haircut with scissors.

Discovery Bottles

Use plastic drink bottles to make these "hands-on" discovery bottles for your science center.*

Muddy Bottle . . . .

Put ½ cup dirt in the bottom of a bottle, and fill it with water. Let the children shake it up and watch the dirt settle. (Try using gravel, peat moss, clay, and different types of soil.)

Collect soil samples from different states or countries and make muddy bottles from them. Label the bottles so the children can compare the soil found in different areas.

Wave Bottle . . . .

Fill the bottle ⅔ full with water. Add several drops of food coloring to the water, then fill it to the top with vegetable oil. Turn the bottle on its side and move it back and forth to make waves.

Magnet Bottle . . . .

Fill the bottle half full with sand or salt. Add pins, paper clips, and small metallic objects to the sand and shake. Let the children take a magnet and try to find the hidden objects.

Bubble Bottle . . . .

Add 1 cup of water, a squirt of dish detergent, and 2 drops of food coloring to the bottle. Shake to make bubbles.

Sound Bottle . . . .

Put beans, popcorn kernels, and rice in different bottles. Stick each bottle inside an old sock. Let the children shake and guess what's in the bottles.

Estimate Bottle . . . .

Put nuts, pebbles, small shells, dried beans, or other small objects in a bottle. After the children guess how many objects are in the bottle, dump out the contents and count them together. (Send this bottle home with the children and let them take turns filling it with objects.)

* Secure the lids of these bottles with a glue gun or super glue.

Density Bottle ·

Take three bottles. Fill one with water, one with vegetable oil, and one with clear shampoo. Add a marble to each bottle, then screw on the lids. The children can observe how the marbles move through different liquids.

Stress Bottle ·

Pour $1/3$ cup clear corn syrup in a bottle. Add glitter, sequins, or small toys. The children can hold the bottle and slowly turn it around. This will help them focus and relax.

Color Bottle ·

Add red food coloring and water to a bottle and label it with the word "red." Make a different color bottle to add to the science center every day.

Seasonal Bottle ·

Put autumn leaves, flowers, nuts, or other natural objects in bottles of water. The children can observe the objects as they disintegrate. (Silk flowers and leaves can also be used.)

Hidden Objects Bottle ·

Fill a bottle $2/3$ full with sand or salt. Add five to ten small objects to the bottle and shake it. Challenge the children to find all of the hidden objects.

Glitter ·

Add glitter, confetti, or crayon shavings to bottles of water.

Seriation ·

Take four or five bottles and put a different amount of water in each one, from empty to full. Mix the bottles up, then let the children seriate them from empty to full.

Squishy Bags

Plastic bags give children the opportunity to observe and investigate a variety of materials and objects.

Materials:

- Ziploc baggies
- shaving cream
- food coloring
- bubble solution
- dirt
- natural objects, such as shells, bones, dead insects, flowers, leaves, etc.
- magnifying glass

Color Bags

Squirt shaving cream into a bag. Add a drop of red and a drop of yellow food coloring. Zip shut. Let the children squeeze the bag to make orange. (Add red and blue to another bag, and yellow and blue to a third bag.)

Bubble Bag

Pour a little commercial or homemade bubble solution in a baggie and let the children squeeze and shake it up.

Muddy Bag

Put dirt in a baggie and add a little water. Play in the mud without getting dirty.

Investigation Bag

Place shells, dead insects, a bird nest, or other natural objects children can explore in baggies. Give them a magnifying glass to enlarge specimens.

Math Center

Children will have opportunities to count, group, make patterns, tell time, measure, explore shapes, make comparisons, and join and separate sets in the math center. Small motor skills, problem-solving, and social skills will also be developed.

Materials:

shelves, table
toy clock
calculator
play money
rulers
tape measure
flannel board
felt shapes and cutouts
popsicle sticks
small toys
geometric shapes
tactile numerals and shapes
puzzles
measuring cups and spoons
Cuisinaire rods
counting cubes
dominoes
dice
deck of cards
geoboard
attribute blocks
paper and pencils
chalkboard
computer
play phone

stop watch, minute timer
number line
pattern blocks
file folder games
bathroom scale
sorting tray or box
balance scale
coins (American and foreign)
objects to count (shells, rocks, buttons, toothpicks, keys, bottle caps, peanuts, pasta, nuts and bolts, paint chips, etc.)

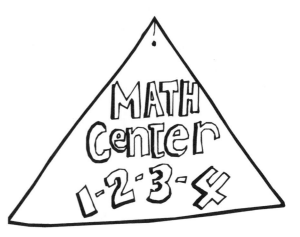

Teacher Tips:

Label baskets, tubs, and clear containers where math manipulatives are stored.

Make math games that integrate themes and concepts you are studying. (Play these as a large group activity, then place them in the math center to encourage small groups of children to play.)

Meaningful Math

Addition and Subtraction
Give children muffin papers and cereal or pretzels to use in working out math problems. (Of course, it's fun to eat them when they're finished.)

One-to-One Correspondence
Have children practice one-to-one correspondence by placing objects in egg cartons, muffin pans, and other separated containers.

Make paper placemats with outlines of dishes and silverware for the children to match up.

Sorting
Use a silverware tray or divided relish dish for sorting activities. In addition, paper sacks, plastic berry baskets, shoe boxes, or paper plates can be used for sorting. Large objects can be sorted into hula hoops.

Counting
Dye pasta as math counters: Separate into 4 plastic bags. Add 1 Tb. rubbing alcohol and a large squirt of food coloring to each bag. Shake. Dry on wax paper.

Birthday candles, party favors, hair bows, leaves, plastic cutlery, blocks, coupons, crayons, and other common classroom objects can also be used for counting and sorting activities.

Small, inexpensive toys that make interesting manipulatives for math are available from The Oriental Trading Company, (800) 228-2269.

Patterns
Make pattern cards by gluing colored toothpicks or pasta onto sentence strips. The children can then reproduce the patterns using the real objects.

Seriation
To make a seriation game, cut cardboard rolls from wrapping paper or paper towels into different lengths.

Size
Add flannel stories such as "Goldilocks and the Three Bears" and "The Three Billy Goats Gruff" to reinforce size comparisons.

Place Value
Draw a line down the middle of a file folder. Write "tens" on the left side and "ones" on the right. Have the children make sets of ten out of popsicle sticks and rubber bands. Children can use bundles of ten and individual sticks to tell place value.

Library

The library should be inviting and interesting, and a place where children fall in love with books. In the library area children can also develop oral language, listening skills, and reading readiness skills while they learn new concepts.

Materials:

- books (all sizes, shapes, subjects)
- comfortable seating (pillows, bean bag chairs, small rocking chairs, etc.)
- book rack and shelves
- Big Books
- magazines
- travel brochures
- flannel board and stories
- puppets
- catalogs
- sensory books
- maps
- picture books
- menus
- dictionary
- letters
- pictures and posters
- class-made books
- listening station
- calendars
- books and tapes
- multilingual children's books
- poems or language experience stories
- newspapers and magazines in different languages and print

Teacher Tips:

Check out books from your public library to add to your classroom.

Encourage parents to donate books and magazines their child no longer uses.

Rather than a holiday gift, request that parents donate a book to your classroom.

Yard sales and thrift stores are good sources for inexpensive books.

Model how to open books, turn pages, and care for them. When books are torn up, involve the children in repairing them.

Let the children help you categorize the books. You might have sections for animal stories, folk tales, nature books, Big Books, etc. Ask the children to draw pictures to use as labels.

Liven Up the Library!

Loft . . . .

Build a reading loft for the library area.
Store books underneath and place pillows
on top.

Book Buddies . . . .

Add "book buddies" (stuffed animals)
children can read to.

Reading Lamp . . . .

Add a small table and lamp the children can
turn on when they want to read.

Reading Pool . . . .

To make a reading pool where children will want to take a dip, fill a plastic
swimming pool with books, pillows, and a quilt.

Tent . . . .

Make a tent in the library with a sleeping bag, flashlight, and books.

Book Nook . . . .

Decorate an appliance box to use as a reading nook.

Puppets . . . .

Make puppets of favorite characters from books so the children can create
their own stories in the library.

Author's Basket . . . .

Add an Author's Basket to your library area. Put all of the
books you have by a particular author in the basket. Add a
label with the author's name and perhaps a photograph on
the handle.

Magazine Rack . . . .

Magazine racks are handy for storing printed materials.
Ask a grocery store manager to save an old rack or a
promotional display you can use.

Tub Time . . . .

Paint an old bath tub and fill it with
pillows and books.

Writing Center

Emergent literacy will flourish in a writing center. Children will develop a positive attitude about school as they work on their reading, writing, vocabulary, social, listening, and small motor skills.

Materials:

table and chairs
pens, pencils, crayons, markers
variety of paper (colored, notepads,
    different shapes and sizes)
carbon paper, tissue paper
envelopes
blank books (fold 2 pieces of paper in
    half and staple)
sticky notes
junk mail
bank deposit slips, magazine inserts,
    book order forms
chalkboard and chalk
wipe-off board and dry markers
manual typewriter
magic slate
stamps and ink pad
scissors, hole punch
glue, tape, stapler

computer and printer
picture file
picture dictionary
magnetic letters
clipboard
used postcards or greeting cards
reading games

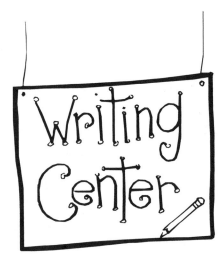

Teacher Tips:

Store writing materials in a shoe rack or desk organizer.
Rotate the paper and materials in the writing center to increase children's interest.
Save samples of what the children do in the writing center to add to their portfolios.

Write On

Class Directory . . . .

Make a class directory so the children can write to their friends. Print each child's name on an index card and glue on his or her picture. Store the cards in a small box, or punch holes in the cards and hang on a metal ring.

Writer's Wall . . . .

Create a Writer's Wall of Fame near the writing center to display children's work.

Word Bank . . . .

Children can use a word bank like a "spell check" to look up words they want to write. You will need a 3" x 5" file box with an alphabetical index. Print sight words, vocabulary words, spelling words, and other words children request on index cards and file them in the box alphabetically.

Sand Tray . . . .

Make a sand tray for children to practice writing letters and words. Glue colorful construction paper in the bottom of a shirt box, then sprinkle 1 to 2 cups of sand or salt over the bottom of the box. Children can trace the letters in the box with their fingers for tactile learning.

School Days . . . .

Add an old school desk to the writing center so the children can play school.

Sensory Play

Sand and water experiences give children sensory pleasure while developing math concepts, small motor skills, social skills, and language.

Materials: . . . .

sand or water table (You can also use your classroom sink,
    plastic tubs, or a wading pool.)
spoons, shovels, pots, pails, watering can
smocks
toy dishes
plastic containers
bottles
measuring cups
funnels
sponges
washable baby dolls, clothes
sifter, strainer
plastic boats, ping pong balls
towel
water wheel
piece of hose, clear tubing
plastic cars and trucks
plastic animals, toys
beaters, eye droppers

Teacher Tips: •

Sensory play should be located on washable flooring near a sink. A bath mat, shower curtain, or drop cloth can also be used to cover the floor.

A hand vacuum cleaner is handy for cleaning up spilled sand or rice. Sponges, mops, and towels will also enable children to clean up after themselves.

Provide smocks for the children to wear when playing in water.

Give children simple rules, such as, "Keep the sand and water in the tub," or "If you spill something, clean it up."

Limit the number of children who can play in the area at one time. Cut feet from colored contact paper and stick them on the floor to indicate the number of children who can play.

Move the sand and water table outside onto the playground in warm weather.

* Remind children to wash their hands before and after playing with sensory materials.

"Sensational" Activities

Creative Materials

For different sensory experiences use birdseed, rice, dried beans, cornmeal, oatmeal, snow, paper confetti, pasta (cooked or raw), cotton balls, dirt, shaving cream, Styrofoam peanuts, leaves, and other natural objects. Mix items together, such as dried beans and rice, cardboard rollers and cornmeal, or sand and seashells.

Individual Play

Put plastic tubs in a wading pool on the floor. Fill the tubs with different items, and the children can sit down and play in their own space. Clear lids from deli trays are good for individual sensory play, too.

Scoop It

Draw faces on ping pong balls with a permanent marker and float them in the water table. Give children a small fish net to scoop them up. Other plastic toys, such as counting bears, can be scooped up with a fish net or picked up with tongs.

Smells and Colors

Add soap bubbles, glitter, food coloring or fragrances (vanilla, mint) to the water table.

Wet Sand

Wet the sand for molding and building sand castles. A spray bottle of water works well for this.

Icebergs

Fill large plastic containers with colored water and freeze to make icebergs. Place the icebergs in the water table with plastic arctic animals.

Sifting

Mix shells and other small objects into the sand. Give children a sieve or strainer to find them. Spray-paint pebbles gold to make "nuggets" the children can pan for.

Magnets

Hide metallic objects such as paper clips and screws in the sand and let children find them with a magnet.

Sink and Float . . . .

Lay out a variety of different objects and ask the children to predict which ones will sink and which ones will float. Have them experiment to see if their predictions are correct.

Rainbow Rice . . . .

Make rainbow rice by mixing 2 tablespoons of rubbing alcohol and a big squirt of food coloring. Pour it into a bag of rice and shake. Dry on wax paper. Dye rice red, blue, yellow, and green, then mix them all together. (This rice can also be used for art projects. Make a design with glue on a sheet of paper, then sprinkle the rainbow rice on it to create a collage.)

Bubbles . . . .

Fill bowls with water and dish detergent. (Dawn and Joy work best.) Give children egg beaters so they can beat up some mountains of bubbles. Fill small cups with a mixture of dish detergent and water; give children straws with which to blow bubbles.

Bath Time . . . .

Let children wash plastic baby dolls and toys with soap and washcloths. They will also have fun washing doll clothes and hanging them up to dry.

Boats . . . .

Children will enjoy experimenting with building boats using aluminum foil, clay, Styrofoam, corks, and sponges. They can glue popsicle sticks together to make rafts, or carve Ivory soap bars with a plastic knife to make a boat.

Mud Pies . . . .

Every child should experience the joy of making mud pies. Mix 4 parts dirt with one part flour. Add enough water so it can be molded like clay. Dry.

Fishing . . . .

Cut fish shapes out of sponges, Styrofoam plates, or colored acetate (plastic report folders or overhead projector sheets). Attach a paper clip to each fish and float the fish in the water. Make a fishing pole to catch them by tying a piece of string to a magnet and a small stick.

Mystery Hands

Children will be delighted with "mystery hands" as they try to identify objects from touch.

Materials: . . . .

- 6 latex gloves
- 1 8½" x 11" piece of cardboard
- large grocery sack
- glue, marker
- sensory materials such as sand, rice, grits, oatmeal, cornmeal, cotton balls, Styrofoam packing, dried beans, cornstarch, and dried leaves.

Directions: . . . .

Fill each glove with one of the items listed above. Tie a knot in the top of the gloves. Label the gloves with their contents. On the cardboard, glue a spoonful of each of the objects in the gloves and label. Put the "mystery hands" in the paper sack. Children can reach into the sack, feel a "hand," and try to identify what is inside it. They can then take out the hand to confirm their guess.

Variations: . . . .

Make two of each mystery hand and put them both in the sack. Children have to feel around until they find the matching hands.

Use the recipes for goop and flubber found on page 159. Pour these mixtures into gloves to make "creepy" hands.

Thinking Station

Critical thinking, problem-solving, and creativity will be
nurtured with these open-ended tasks.

Estimating

Materials:

- clear jar
- small objects (candy, nuts, beads, crayons, coins, etc.)
- paper, pencils

Directions:

Fill the jar with different objects. Ask the children to guess how many
objects are in the jar and write their answers on pieces of paper. Count
the objects at the end of the day to see whose guess was closest.

Mystery Object

Materials:

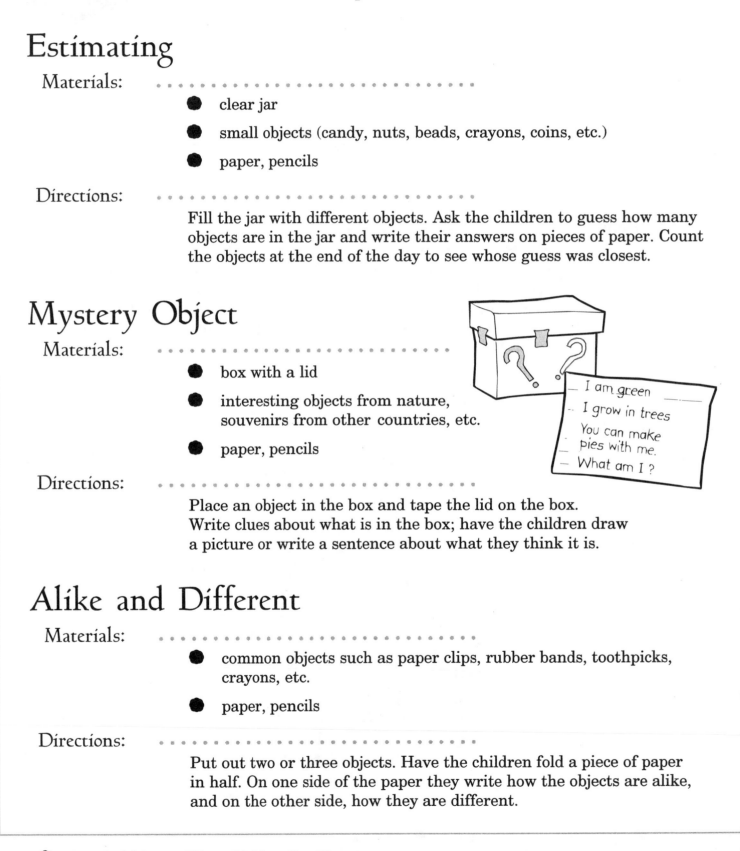

- box with a lid
- interesting objects from nature,
  souvenirs from other countries, etc.
- paper, pencils

I am green
I grow in trees
You can make pies with me.
What am I ?

Directions:

Place an object in the box and tape the lid on the box.
Write clues about what is in the box; have the children draw
a picture or write a sentence about what they think it is.

Alike and Different

Materials:

- common objects such as paper clips, rubber bands, toothpicks,
  crayons, etc.
- paper, pencils

Directions:

Put out two or three objects. Have the children fold a piece of paper
in half. On one side of the paper they write how the objects are alike,
and on the other side, how they are different.

What Would You Do?

Materials: . . . .

- interesting magazine pictures or photographs
- tape recorder

Directions: . . . .

Display one of the pictures and ask the children to dictate a story about it into the tape recorder. They can also pretend they are one of the characters in the picture and tell a story.

Invention

Materials: . . . .

- recycled materials (boxes, bottle caps, Styrofoam pieces, foil, cans, etc.)
- tape, scissors, glue, paper scraps

Directions: . . . .

Put out the objects and have the children make new inventions.

Brainstorm

Materials: . . . .

- items that relate to a season or unit of study, such as a pumpkin, magnet, wheel, etc.
- paper, pencils

Directions: . . . .

Place a unique object in the thinking station and ask the children to make a list of all the different ways it could be used.

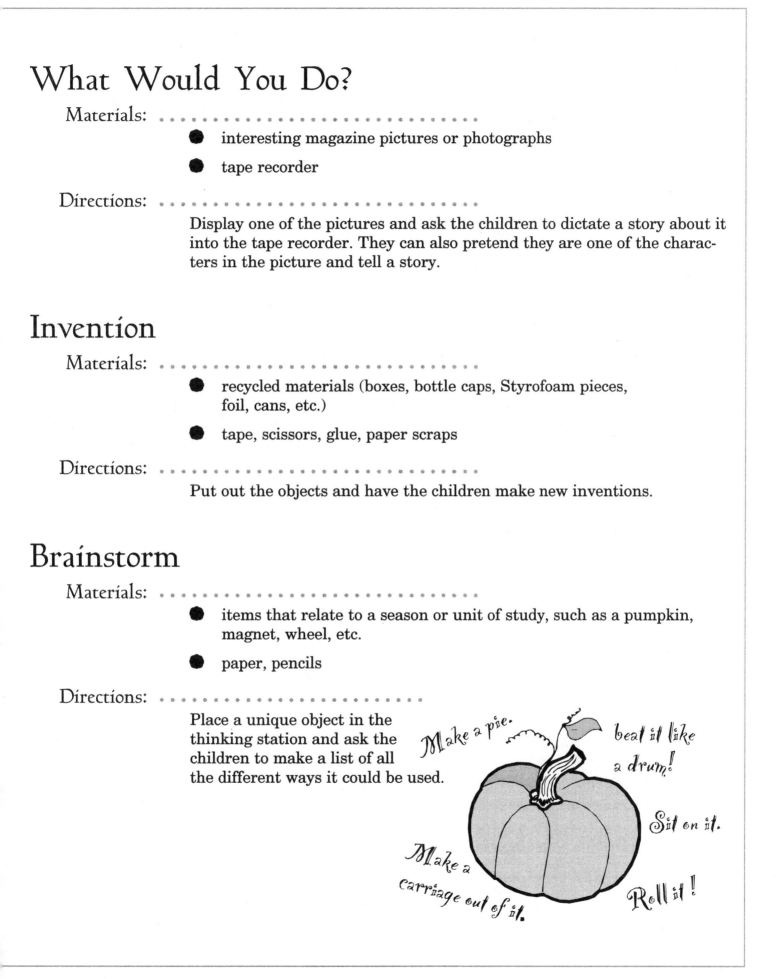

Make a pie.

beat it like a drum!

Sit on it.

Make a carriage out of it.

Roll it!

Music Center

Through music children can improve auditory skills, verbal expression, motor skills, creativity, and social skills while they derive personal enjoyment.

Materials:

musical instruments
ethnic instruments
homemade instruments
record player
records
keyboard
autoharp
tone bells
xylophone
tape recorder/tapes
piano
musical toys
music box
radio
listening station
visuals for songs
puppets
international music
scarves, ribbon streamers
instruments from other countries
song books
sheet music

Teacher Tips:

Hang rhythm instruments from hooks on the back of a shelf or a pegboard.

Model how to play the instruments so the children can make music and not noise.

Take instruments outside and have a parade.

Put a green piece of tape on the "play" button and a red piece of tape on the "stop" button to help children use the tape recorder independently.

Tin Pan Band

Drums . . . .

Make drums from oatmeal boxes, canisters, boxes, and coffee cans.

Drumsticks . . . .

Drumsticks can be made by wrapping cloth (5" circles) around cotton balls at the end of a pencil. Rubberband in place.

Guitar . . . .

Make a guitar by stretching rubber bands over the opening of a cardboard box and plucking.

Cymbals . . . .

Pie pans or paper plates can be used as cymbals to make a soft sound.

Bells . . . .

String bells on elastic and knot ends; wear on wrists or ankles. You can also string bells to ponytail holders with bread ties.

Rhythm Sticks . . . .

Use paper towel rolls as rhythm sticks.

Shakers . . . .

Put dried beans, rice, popcorn kernels, or pasta in plastic jars, bottles, film containers, frosting cans, or small milk jugs to make shakers.

Hand Rattles . . . .

Cut a 1½" slit in a tennis ball with a knife. Squeeze the sides to open the hole, then insert beans or small pebbles. Shake for a soft sound.

Tambourines . . . .

Glue or staple two paper plates together $\frac{2}{3}$ of the way around. Put a few beans or popcorn kernels in the middle, then staple the opening closed. Decorate with markers and crepe paper streamers.

Kazoos . . . .

Kazoos are fun to make for the whole class. Poke 3 holes in the side of a cardboard toilet paper roll with a pencil. Wrap wax paper over one end and rubberband in place. Hum a tune into the other end.

Sand Blocks . . . .

Glue sandpaper to blocks of wood. Hold a block in each hand and slide them back and forth against each other.

Xylophone . . . .

Cut wrapping paper rolls into different lengths and play with a wooden spoon.

Water Bells . . . .

Fill glasses or glass drink bottles with different amounts of water. Strike them with a metal spoon to create different sounds.

Rainstick . . . .

To make a rainstick, purchase a mailing tube at the post office. Let children hammer roofing nails into the tube. (Make sure the nails you use are shorter than the diameter of the mailing tube.) Fill with rice, dried beans, and aquarium gravel. Glue the lids onto the tubes. Decorate with markers, crayons, or paint. Slowly rotate the tube back and forth to make the sound of rain.

"Reading" Notes . . . .

Purchase a set of colored tone bells. Use crayons with colors that match the tone bells to make dots that when played will be simple songs.

Large Motor Center

(Indoor or Outdoor)

In the large motor area children develop coordination, strength, large muscles, physical fitness, social skills; they also can release energy and frustrations.

Materials: ··································

balls (large, medium, small)
balance beam
bean bags
climbing equipment
hula hoops
tumbling mats
play gym
slide
record player or tape recorder
parachute
jump rope
riding toys
scarves

Teacher Tips: ●●●

If space is available indoors, a special area for motor activity will be enjoyed by children. This should be set up away from quiet areas so children won't disturb each other.

Limit the number of children who can play in the center at a particular time.

Give simple guidelines for using the equipment. Make rebus cards that will help the children remember the rules.

Fun and Games

Bean Bags ....

Make a bean bag by filling an old sock with a cup of dried beans. Wrap a rubber band around the middle of the sock, and pull the cuff of the sock over it to make a bean bag. (For younger children, fill the sock with cotton balls or Styrofoam peanuts so they won't hurt each other when they throw them.)

Tossing Box ....

Toss bean bags into holes cut in a box. (Children can also toss bean bags or balls into a laundry basket or trash can.)

Catch Can ....

Give children a potato chip canister. Let them bounce tennis balls and try to catch them in the can.

Paper Balls ....

Make paper balls by wadding up scrap paper and wrapping masking tape around it.

Space Ball ....

Cut off one leg of a pair of pantyhose from the knee down. Stuff the remainder of the pantyhose in that toe and tie a knot around it. Throw it in the air and you have a space ball.

Hand Ball ....

Staple 2 paper plates together ¾" of the way around. Insert the hand in the hole and you have a paddle you can use to play handball with a paper ball.

Hose Ball ·

Cut off the foot from a pair of pantyhose. Stuff the pantyhose down into that toe and knot around it to make a ball. Trim off the excess.

Basketball

Hoop ·

Stretch a coat hanger into a circle. Tie on 18" strips of plastic ribbon or strips out from fabric. Bend the hook of the hanger down over a door or drawer to hang it. Use hose balls, paper balls, or small foam balls to toss into the hoop.

Tunnels ·

Cut both ends off of several cardboard boxes and join the boxes together with tape. Children will enjoy crawling through this long tunnel.

Ribbon Wands ·

Children can make their own ribbon wands for dancing by stapling 3' pieces of ribbon or crepe paper to straws.

Driver's License ·

Cut poster board into 3" x 4" pieces for the children to make driver's licenses they can use when "driving" a riding toy. Have them draw their pictures and write their names, birthdays, addresses, phone numbers, and physical descriptions.

Balance Beam ·

Put a piece of tape on the floor, or lay a piece of 2" x 4" lumber on the floor, to make a balance beam children can walk on.

Construction

(Indoor and Outdoor)

Construction opportunities enhance motor skills, independence, creativity, problem-solving, math concepts, and self-confidence.

Materials:

workbench
safety goggles
carpenter's apron
tools (hammer, screwdriver, saw, pliers)*
nails, screws
wire, string
rubber bands
tape (masking, cloth, and transparent)
paper, pencils
glue
scissors
ruler, tape measure
blueprints
cardboard boxes
popsicle sticks
Styrofoam packing (large pieces)

wood scraps (available from building supply center or construction site)
paint, brushes
sandpaper
cardboard rollers (from toilet paper and paper towels)
clothespins
wooden dowels
spools

* Teach tool safety and supervise the children carefully.

Teacher Tips:

Vary the tools and materials according to the age and ability of the children.

Organize the materials in tubs, ice cream buckets, or baskets and label the contents for easy clean up.

Offer building experiences indoors and outdoors when the weather is warm.

Creative Construction

Hammering . . . .

Let children hammer nails in an old tree stump. For younger children, drive the nails in half way and let them finish pounding them in.

Golf Tees . . . .

Children can hammer golf tees into the ground or into large pieces of Styrofoam with a plastic hammer.

Sanding . . . .

Give children wood scraps and sandpaper and let them sand blocks that can be used in the block area or for art projects.

Tin Punch . . . .

Tin designs can be made by hammering nails in aluminum pie pans.

Clubhouse . . . .

Plastic milk crates, bricks, pallets, boards, old tires, and blankets can be used to build a clubhouse.

Cardboard Castles . . . .

Cardboard castles can be constructed with recycled food boxes, corrugated cardboard boxes, cardboard tubes, and masking tape.

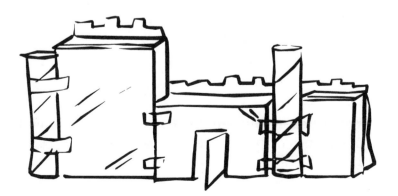

Surprise Center

What a refreshing idea for a rotating center in your classroom! Use children's interests, classroom themes, or holidays as a springboard for this center. It should be fun, open-ended, and designed to meet the children's developmental needs. Provide enough materials to interest and challenge the children, but don't overwhelm them. (Locate the surprise center in a designated area of the classroom so children will know it's an area where there will be changes.)

Cutting Caboose

Materials:

- large appliance box (large enough to hold 2 chairs)
- scissors, scrap paper
- 2 small chairs
- red paint, brushes
- black construction paper

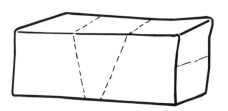

Directions:

Cut a door out of the box similar to the one illustrated. Let the children paint the box red, then cut out four black paper circles and glue them onto the box for wheels. Place two chairs in the box facing each other. Tie a pair of scissors to each chair, then tape on a file folder with scrap paper. The children sit in the chairs facing each other and "cut away" in the "cutting caboose."

Variations:

For younger children, create a "tearing train" and give them old magazines or paper they can tear into little pieces.

Wrapping Station

Materials:

- gift boxes, inexpensive wrapping paper, tissue paper, funny papers, tape, scissors, ribbon, paper, pens, envelopes, old greeting cards

Directions:

Let the children wrap the boxes and decorate them with ribbons and cards.

Milk A Cow

Materials:

- 2 chairs, broom handle, latex glove, pail, tape, string

Directions:

Tape the broom handle to two chairs. To make the udder, fill the glove with water. Poke holes with a pin in the fingers of the glove and tie it to the middle of the broomstick. Let children "milk" the cow by squeezing the glove over the pail.

Variations:

Make a cardboard head for the cow, then tie on a rope for a tail. You can also make a fence and add hay.

Shoe Match

Materials: ●

● Different kinds of shoes (men's, children's, babies', ladies', work shoes, house shoes, sports shoes, etc.)

Directions: ●

Mix up the shoes, then let children match the ones that belong together.

Variations: ●

Add shoe polish and rags so children can shine shoes.

Give children different kinds of socks to sort.

Picnic Party

Materials: ●

● picnic basket, tablecloth, play food, paper products, radio, sunglasses, empty bottles and food boxes

Directions: ●

Let children pretend they are going on a picnic.

Variations: ●

Add birthday party favors, paper products, etc.

Beauty/Barber Shop

Materials: ●

● vanity mirror, curlers, hair dryers and curling irons (cut the cords off old ones), ribbons, barrettes, combs, brushes, empty shampoo and hair spray bottles, nail polish bottles (filled with water), empty make-up containers

Directions: ●

Let children take turns fixing each other's hair.

Variations: ●

Let children pretend to shave with popsicle sticks and shaving cream.

Rain Forest

Materials: ....

- books, rainsticks, stuffed animals (monkeys, birds, etc.),
  paper vines hanging down,
  tape of a rain forest, drums

Directions: ....

Children can visit a rain forest
by exploring the objects and books.

Computer City

Materials: ....

- old computer keyboards (cut cords off back),
  paper, pencils, play phone, calculators, calendars,
  computer paper

Directions: ....

Children can pretend to be in an office as they become familiar with a
keyboard.

Giggles and Squiggles

Materials: ....

- Styrofoam peanuts, foam packing, Styrofoam trays, popsicle sticks,
  toothpicks, pipe cleaners, egg cartons, tape, pictures of modern art

Directions: ....

Let children create sculptures with the recycled objects.

Fitness Center

Materials: ....

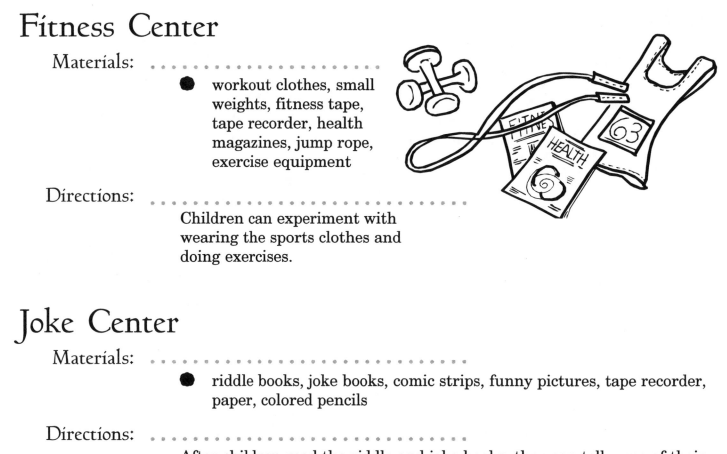

- workout clothes, small weights, fitness tape, tape recorder, health magazines, jump rope, exercise equipment

Directions: ....

Children can experiment with wearing the sports clothes and doing exercises.

Joke Center

Materials: ....

- riddle books, joke books, comic strips, funny pictures, tape recorder, paper, colored pencils

Directions: ....

After children read the riddle and joke books, they can tell some of their own jokes into the tape recorder or draw their own comics.

Holiday Happenings

Adapt the surprise center to seasons and holidays. *Weave a Basket, Mask Makers, Salute to America,* and *Healthy Harvest* are a few ideas.

Game Time

Acontinual dilemma for teachers is how to ensure children develop necessary skills, while providing them with creative and meaningful learning opportunities.

Curriculum objectives and lists of basic skills will not go away, but these fun games will add a little more interest and challenge to the process of meeting these goals.

The games in this section can be used as choice activities in centers, with small groups of children who need additional help, or with a large group whenever you have a few extra minutes to reinforce skills.

In addition, parents could check these games out to work with their children at home, or you could plan a workshop for parents so they could construct some of their own games.

Consider these tips in making games:

- Keep games short and simple by focusing on one concept or skill.

- Make games colorful, attractive, and neat. Laminate or cover with clear contact paper to protect them.

- Try to make games where all children will have fun and win.

- Adapt games to be simpler or more challenging to meet the unique needs of your students.

- Make self-contained games that can be stored in zipper bags, clasp envelopes, file folders, boxes, bags, or tubs.

- Demonstrate how to play the games, then offer support until the children have become familiar with the directions.

- Provide children with a wide variety of games for large group, small group, and individual play.

Lucky Stars

Construct this game with activities children can do if they finish their work or "can't think of anything to do."

Materials:

- coffee can or oatmeal can
- construction paper cut in star shapes
- fine tip markers

Directions:

Cut out stars from the construction paper and write one of the activities below on each star. Place the stars in the can and tell the children they can choose a "lucky star" if they need something to do.

Activities:

Read a book.
Write a letter to a friend.
Play a board game.
Make a gift for someone in the art area.
Work a puzzle.
Build a castle with the blocks.
Help a friend.
Do some exercises.
Make a book.
Do a job for your teacher.
Paint a picture of yourself.
Make a pet you'd like with play dough.
Put on a puppet show.
Find a friend and draw a picture together.
Look out the window.
Sing a song.

Variations:

Adapt these activities to the interests and abilities of the children in your classroom.

Ask the children to contribute fun ideas to the "lucky star" can.

Decorate the "lucky star" can with glitter or stickers.

Funny Ears

This self-checking game enables children to correct themselves and learn independently.

Materials: . . . .

- construction paper
- bunny pattern on the following page
- scissors
- markers

Directions: . . . .

Cut out 10 to 15 bunnies using the pattern on the following page. Draw faces on them and fold over their right ear as shown. Write a math fact on the body of each bunny. Print the answer under its right ear. Children play the game by saying the answer to the math problem, then checking under the bunny's ear to verify their answer.

Variations: . . . .

Number the bunnies, then have the children number their papers and write the answer for each question.

For younger children, put spots on the bunnies; have them count the spots and check the correct number under the bunny's ear.

Put pictures on the bunnies and ask the children to identify the initial consonant sound. Write the correct letter under each bunny's ear.

Alphagories

Letters, beginning sounds, and parts of speech are all reinforced with this challenging game.

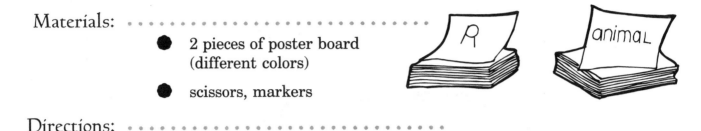

Materials:

- 2 pieces of poster board (different colors)
- scissors, markers

Directions:

Cut each piece of poster board into twenty-four 4" squares. On one set of squares print the letters of the alphabet. (Print "xyz" on one square.) Write the following categories on the other set of squares:

title of a book	body part
color	game or sport
famous person	something outside
television show	song title
animal	toy
something that flies	something in the school
fruit or vegetable	plant
city or town	country or state
type of transportation	action
occupation	river, lake, or ocean
machine	piece of clothing
food	restaurant or store

Tell the children that you will draw a card from each pile. They have to try and think of a word that begins with the letter on one card and fits the category on the other card. After children have practiced playing the game several times, divide them into teams and play. Give the team that comes up with a response first the point. (Shuffle cards between each round to create new possibilities.)

Variations:

Allow small groups of children to play Alphagories and compete individually.

Me Blocks

In addition to contributing to children's positive sense of self, these blocks can be used for math activities, songs, stories, and building.

Materials:

- milk or juice cartons (pint size works best)
- photographs of the children
- construction paper
- scissors, glue, markers or crayons
- clear contact paper or packaging tape

Directions:

Each child will need two cartons. First, have the children wash them out and dry them. Cut the cartons so they are 3½" tall. Squeeze the sides of one carton so it will fit into the other to form a block. Glue the child's picture to one side, then cover the other sides with squares of construction paper. Let the children decorate the sides with crayons or markers. Cover the blocks with clear contact or packaging tape for long use.

Variations:

Let the children count the blocks or use them for telling number stories. (For example, "There were two friends playing and three more came along. How many were there in all?")

Sing songs with the children's blocks. (For example, hold up different blocks as you sing this song to the tune of "Skip to My Lou:"

> *"Hello, (child's name), how are you?*
> *Hello, (child's name), how are you?*
> *Hello, (child's name), how are you?*
> *How are you this morning?"*

Cut out pictures from magazines of different kinds of people and use them to make "people blocks."

Send home directions for these blocks as a project for parents to do with their children.

Muffin Man

Sing a song, play a game, and learn, all at the same time!

Materials: . . . .

● different colors of construction paper

Directions: . . . .

Have the children sit in a circle. Hold up one color at a time and sing this song below to the tune of "Do You Know the Muffin Man?"

> ***Do you see the color blue,***
> ***The color blue, the color blue?***
> ***Do you see the color blue***
> ***Somewhere in the room?***

Choose a child to point to an object that color in the room as he or she sings back to you:

> ***Yes, I see the color blue,***
> ***The color blue, the color blue.***
> ***Yes, I see the color blue***
> ***Somewhere in the room.***

Continue holding up different colors and singing about them as the children point to objects in the room.

Variations: . . . .

Use letters, numerals, words, or shapes in place of colors in the song and have the children find them in the classroom.

Handy Signs

Children will be exposed to manual communication and how people who are hearing-impaired talk to each other with their hands.

Materials:

- copy of the American Manual Alphabet (see following page)
- poster board
- markers
- index cards
- scissors, glue

Directions:

Enlarge two copies of the signs on the following page on a copy machine. Glue one set onto the poster board. Cut apart the hand signs of the other set and glue them onto index cards. Shuffle up the cards and place them face down on the table. One child at a time draws a card, makes the sign with her hand, then tries to match the sign on the index card with the one on the poster. Have the children continue drawing the cards until all of the letters have been identified.

Variations:

Challenge the children to learn how to spell their names in sign.

Let the children practice spelling words by signing them.

Teach children other signs for common phrases or songs.

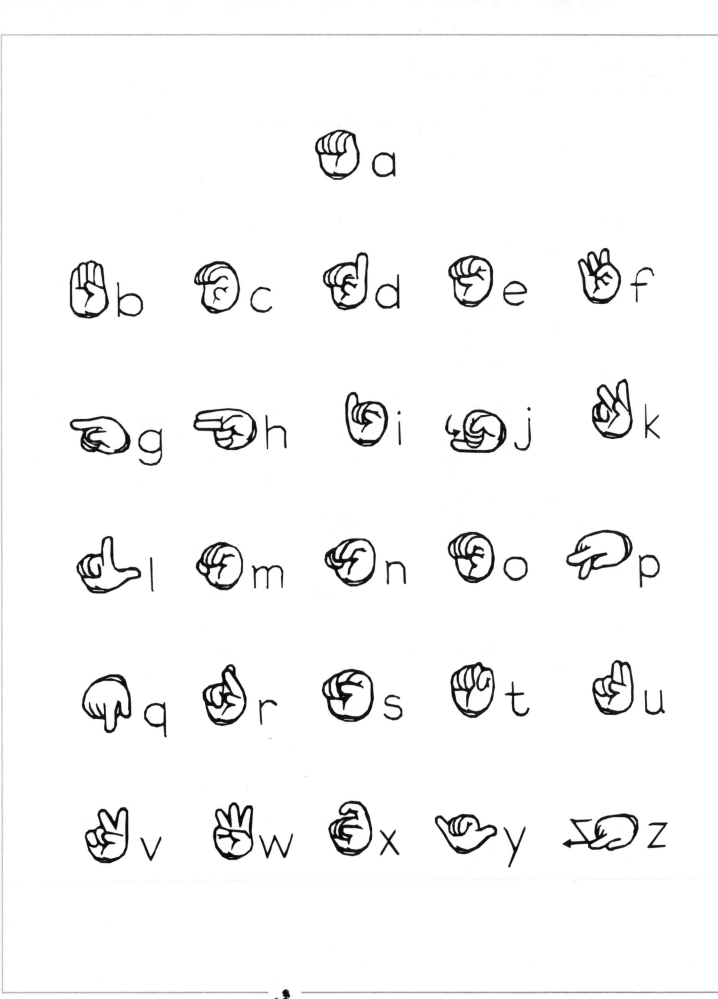

Catch a Whale by the Tail

Children will have a whale of fun learning with this game!

Materials: . . . .

- cardboard roller from a pants hanger
- magnet (horseshoe magnets work well)
- construction paper, scissors
- paper clips
- string or yarn (24" long)

Directions: . . . .

Cut out whales from the construction paper using the pattern below. Print a different letter on each whale. Attach a paper clip to the tail of each whale. To make a fishing pole, tie one end of the string to the cardboard roller, and tie the other end of the string to the magnet. Spread the whales out on the floor. The children take turns trying to catch a whale by the tail with the fishing pole. After catching it, they can identify the letter on it.

Variations: . . . .

Print numerals, sight words, or math facts on the whales.

Shop and Save

Coupons can be used for sorting, numeral recognition, addition, and multiplication.

Materials:

- coupons from newspapers and store advertisements
- lunch sacks
- scissors, markers, glue
- coupon pouch or billfold

Directions:

Ask the children to cut out coupons from the newspapers and advertisements. Print corresponding values in cents on the lunch sacks as shown. Have the children take the coupons and sort them into the appropriate sacks. Store the coupons in a pouch or billfold.

Variations:

Sort coupons into different categories, such as "foods" and "non-foods."

Ask older children to add the coupons to see how much money they could save. How much would they save if it were double or triple coupon day?

Give children a certain amount of money to spend on food for their family for a week; have them look at a grocery store advertisement and make a shopping list.

Use menus from restaurants for children to see what they could order for $5.00 or another specified amount.

Flip Flop

Children won't realize they are learning letters, numerals, and other skills as they flip these burgers.

Materials:

- poster board
- scissors, markers
- spatula
- Ziploc bag

Directions:

Cut out hamburgers from the poster board using the pattern below. On the front of each hamburger write a math fact. On the back write the answer. Children lay out the hamburgers on the floor or a table. They read the problem and say the answer, then take the spatula and flip over the hamburger to see if they are correct.

Variations:

Use this game for identifying upper- and lower-case letters, sets, numerals, beginning sounds, alphabetical order, antonyms, and other skills.

Face Graphing

This activity will provide children with a very concrete way to graph and make comparisons.

Materials: ·

- paper plates
- crayons, markers
- bulletin board paper

Directions: ·

Ask each child to decorate his paper plate to look like his face. Place two large sheets of bulletin board paper on the floor. On the top of one write the word "cats" and draw a cat. On the other write the word "dogs" and draw a dog. Have the children sit on the floor with their paper-plate faces. Ask them to decide which animal is their favorite between a cat and a dog, then have them place their faces under the appropriate picture. When all the children have placed their plates in one of the categories, ask the children which one has more. Count the plates on both sides to verify their guess. Use the plate faces for other comparisons, such as their favorite food, how many people are in their family, how many teeth they've lost, their favorite color, their favorite character in a story, and so forth.

Variations: ·

Have the children make smaller faces on 2" circles to use on a graph made on a piece of poster board.

Use leaves, blocks, crayons, and other common objects to make graphs.

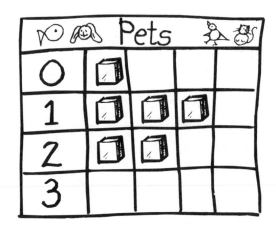

Let's Go to School

(A Community Board Game)

Map making and community pride are enhanced with a board game that reflects the children's neighborhood.

Materials:

- poster board
- markers, crayons
- small animals
- 1 die or a pair of dice

Directions:

Involve the children in making a map of their school community. Small groups of children might do this in the block center, on the chalkboard, or on large pieces of newsprint. Incorporate the children's ideas of the important places in their neighborhood in drawing a board game, similar to the one below, on the poster board. Let the children decorate it with markers or crayons.

To play the game, each child chooses an animal and puts it on "Home." Children take turns rolling the dice and moving their animal that number of spaces. The first one to reach the school wins.

Variations:

Divide older children into groups and let them make their own community board games.

Incorporate math and reading flash cards into the game.

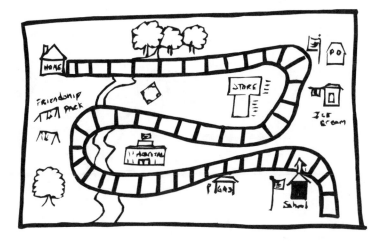

Word Hunt

Sight words will be easy to learn with this word hunt.

Materials:

- sentence strips or index cards
- marker or crayon
- tape
- pointer (yardstick, paper wand, etc.)

Directions:

Choose five sight words you would like the children to learn. Write each sight word five times on index cards or sentence strips. Tape four copies of each word around the room on the walls, cabinets, windows, door, ceiling, etc. Gather the children and ask them if they've seen some words hidden around the room. Hold up one word at a time and read it together with the children. Tell the children to raise their hands if they can find that same word hidden in the room. Let children have turns taking the pointer and finding the word in the room. Encourage them to read the word as they point to it. Continue finding other hidden words.

Variations:

Hide spelling words for the children to find each week.

Make a list of words found in the classroom and photocopy it. Children can put the list on a clipboard, go around the room, and check off the words as they find them.

Let the children go on a "letter hunt" or "numeral hunt" by finding different letters and numerals in the classroom and pointing to them.

Cut out a star pattern from construction paper and staple it to a straw to make a pointer.

and

go

is

you

Piece of Pie

A pizza pie is good to eat, but it can also be a clever learning tool for children.

Materials: ....
- round cardboard from pizza
- markers, ruler
- clothespins (spring-type)

Directions: ....

Divide the pizza cardboard into eight pie shapes. Color each section a different color. Color eight clothespins corresponding colors. Have the children clip clothespins onto the appropriate color.

Variations: ....

Write color words on the clothespins for the children to match.

Put different sets of sausage (small red circles) on the pie shapes and write numerals on the clothespins for the children to match.

Print math problems on the pizza slices and write the answers on the clothespins.

Color pizza cardboards to look like pies and cut them into fraction puzzles. Label similar cardboards as shown so the children can match them up.

Name Bingo

Children will recognize letters and learn how to spell their names with this adaptation of Bingo.

Materials:

- sentence strips or heavy paper cut 3" x 20"
- 3" x 5" index cards
- markers, scissors
- box or bag
- beans, Styrofoam chips, or other objects to use as markers

Directions:

Write each child's first and last name in large letters on a sentence strip. Print the letters of the alphabet on the index cards. Distribute the name cards to the children, along with beans, Styrofoam, or other objects to use as markers. Put the letters in a box or bag. Pull out one letter at a time and hold it up for the children to see. If the children have that letter in their names, they cover it up with one of their markers. (If letters appear more than once, they cover them all.) When the children cover all the letters in their names, they yell, "Bingo." The game continues until each child has covered up the letters in his name.

Variations:

Play a similar game to help children learn their phone numbers. Print each child's phone number on a sentence strip; print individual numerals from 0 to 9 on index cards. Children may cover up the numerals on their phone number as they are drawn.

Use cereal or crackers as markers, then let the children eat them as a treat.

Memory Games

Memory games are excellent for developing visual memory, reading skills, and attention span.

Materials:

- poster board cut in 3½" squares
- stickers (2 of each)

Directions:

Make matching cards by putting two like stickers on the squares. Mix up the cards and put them face down on the floor or a table. One child at a time chooses two squares and turns them over. If the stickers match, then that child may keep the pair and have another turn. If they don't match, the child has to turn them over and the next child gets a turn. The game continues until all the pairs of cards have been matched.

Variations:

To introduce this game, use four pairs of cards. As the children improve, increase the number of pairs used in the game.

Get two of the same toy catalogs or store advertisements and cut out matching objects to use in making memory cards. Coupons, food labels, and logos also make interesting memory games.

Use Old Maid cards to play memory games.

Make memory games where children must match up sight words, upper- and lower-case letters, sets and numerals, or like shapes.

Movable Alphabet

With these letter blocks children will see how letters can be put together to build words, and words can be put together to build sentences.

Materials:

- unit blocks
- tagboard
- tape, scissors, markers

Directions:

Cut the tagboard into 2½" squares to fit on the smallest unit blocks. Write alphabet letters on the squares, and tape one onto each block. (Make two of letters frequently used, such as a, e, i, o, l, s, t.) Demonstrate how you can take the letter blocks and put them together to "build" words. Encourage the children to make the individual sound of the letter on each block, then blend the sounds together to read the words.

Variations:

Make word families that the children can read by changing the first letter in words such as can, run, pot, like, make, pin, town, bat, pet, run, etc.

Let the children use these blocks to make spelling words or vocabulary words.

Cut the tagboard into 2½" x 5" rectangles and write sight words on them. Tape these to larger unit blocks. Put the word blocks together to build sentences that the children can read.

Doughnut Holes

You can't eat these doughnuts, but children will enjoy playing with them just the same.

Materials: . . . .

- construction paper
- scissors, markers
- zipper bag

Directions: . . . .

Cut out ten doughnuts and holes using the patterns below. On each doughnut write a number word. On each hole write a matching numeral. Children take the doughnut holes and match them up to the appropriate doughnut. Store the doughnuts and holes in a zipper bag.

Variations: . . . .

Put dots (chocolate chips) on the doughnuts and matching numerals on the holes.

Use this format for matching upper and lowercase letters.

For younger children, cut doughnuts out of different kinds of wallpaper and have them match up like patterns.

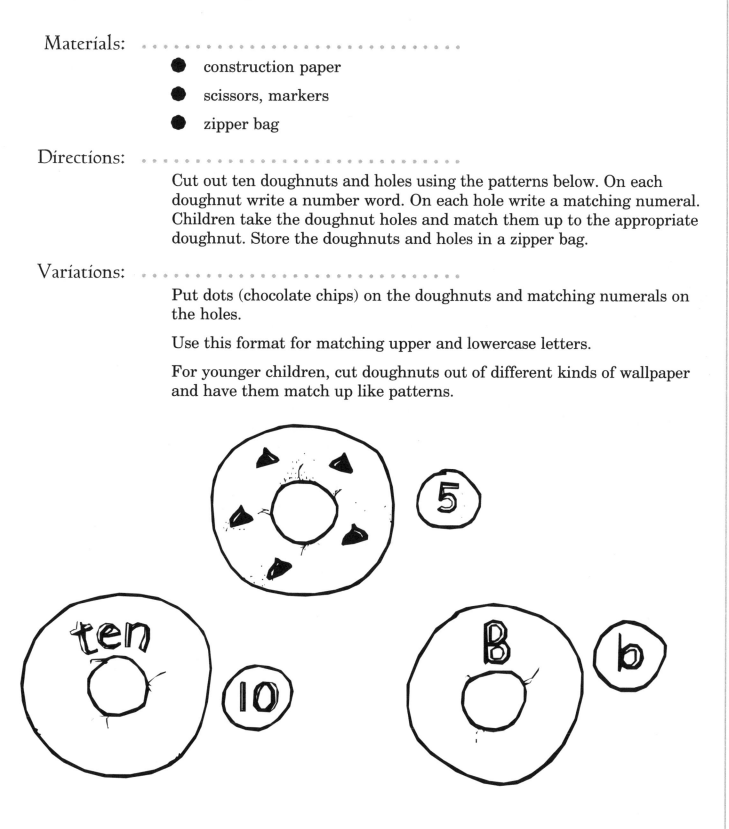

Doodle Bug

This game can reinforce math and reading skills, while children use their small motor skills in a creative way.

Materials:

- poster board cut 14" x 10"
- copy of the game board from the following page
- glue
- paper, pencils
- heavy paper cut in 2½" x 4" rectangles (25)
- caps from dried up magic markers

Directions:

Glue the game board on the following page onto the poster board. On the rectangular cards write sight words, math equations, letters or other facts. Also make one, two, or three dots on each card as shown. Players choose a magic marker cap and put it on "Start". Each player will also need a pencil and a piece of paper.

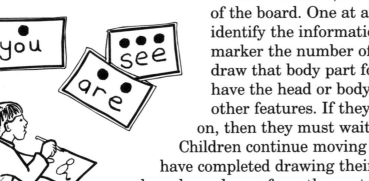

Shuffle the cards, and put them face down in the middle of the board. One at a time children draw a card and identify the information on it. They may then move their marker the number of dots indicated on the card and draw that body part for their "doodlebug." (They must have the head or body before they can draw the legs and other features. If they can't use the body part they land on, then they must wait until their next turn to draw.) Children continue moving around the game board until they have completed drawing their "doodlebug." (When all the cards have been drawn from the center of the board, shuffle them up and begin again.)

Variations:

For older children, write questions on the cards that relate to a unit of study, current events, or literature that they have read.

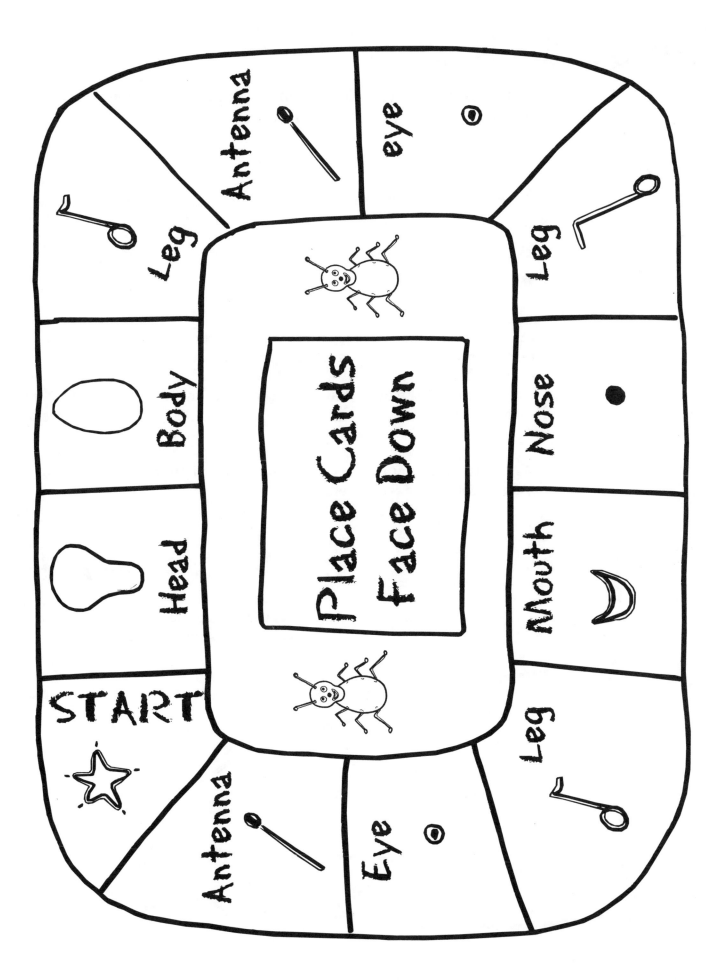

Sneakers

Sneakers is an excellent game for matching upper- and lower-case letters, colors, or sets and numerals.

Materials:

- construction paper
- markers, scissors
- clothespins (spring type)
- zipper bag

Directions:

Cut out several pairs of sneakers from construction paper using the pattern below. On one shoe, print an upper-case letter, and on another shoe, print the matching lower-case letter. Mix up all the shoes, and ask the children to sort the ones that belong together by putting a clothespin on each pair.

Variations:

Write numerals and number words on shoes, pictures and beginning sounds, colors and words, etc.

Show Time

Show Time encourages children to focus on skills, and can be a valuable tool for teachers to use in assessment.

Materials:

- 3" x 5" index cards
- envelopes
- markers

Directions:

Make a set of numeral cards for each child by writing the numerals from 0 to 10 on the index cards. Have the children put their numeral cards in an envelope and print their name on the front. To play "Show Time," ask the children to lay out their cards in front of them. Tell them to hold up different numerals as you call them out. (This enables the teacher to quickly observe children who are weak in this area.) The teacher can also snap their fingers or clap a certain number of times, and ask the children to hold up the appropriate numeral.

Variations:

To reinforce addition and subtraction, call out a math fact and have the children hold up the answer. Make up word problems and ask the children to "show" you the answer.

For younger children, start with the numerals 1 to 5. For older children, use higher numbers.

To review consonant sounds, print letters on index cards and have children hold up the sound they hear when you call out different words.

Where Is Mousie?

Mousie can hide under letters, numerals, or words, which children learn as they look for him.

Materials:

- poster board cut in 8" squares
- gray construction paper
- scissors, markers

Directions:

Cut out a small mouse using the pattern below. On the poster board print sight words. Have the children sit on the floor in a circle. Ask them to read the words as you place them on the floor in the middle of the circle. Tell the children to turn around and close their eyes as you hide Mousie under one of the words. When children turn back around repeat this chant:

> ***Mousie, Mousie, where can you be?***
> ***Mousie, Mousie, let's peek and see!***

Choose one child to guess where Mousie is hiding. The child says the word, then peeks under it to see if Mousie is there. The game continues until someone finds the mouse. That person may then hide Mousie.

Variations:

Print numerals, letters, different shapes, or other information on the cards. Make a paper turkey, jack-o-lantern, snowflake, heart, or other symbol to relate to a season or holiday to hide under the cards.

am	Help	he
of	like	to
make	has	she

Alligator

Don't let the alligator catch you not paying attention in this game!

Materials:

- can with a smooth edge (potato stick and drink mix cans work well)
- white poster board cut in 5" x 2" rectangles
- markers, scissors, glue
- green construction paper

Directions:

Cut 30 rectangles from the poster board. Print the letters of the alphabet on the bottom of 26 of them. On the other four draw a small alligator similar to the one at the bottom of the page. Cover the can with green construction paper and "alligator eyes," as shown. Mix up the cards, then put them all in the can. (Letters should be placed in the bottom of the can.) Explain that you will pass the alligator can around and everyone can draw out a card. If they get a card with a letter, they should say the name of the letter. If they get an alligator, they should yell, "Alligator," and everyone else must stand up and run in place. Start the game with this rhyme:

> *There's a big, bad alligator sneaking up on you,*
> *And he's going to take a bite if you don't know*
> *   what to do.*
> *So open up your eyes and ears and do what I say.*
> *Are you ready? Get set! Let's play!*

Continue playing the game until all the cards have been drawn. Mix them up and begin all over again.

Variations:

Have the children think of words that begin with the letters they draw.

Draw shapes or colors on the cards for younger children, and write numerals, math facts, and sight words for older students.

Change the game so whoever draws the alligator is "out" of the game. The last one left wins.

Quiz Time

This simple game can be used for reinforcing many concepts, and can be adapted to different skill levels.

Materials:

- 3" x 5" index cards
- golf tees
- hole punch
- fine tip markers
- zipper bag

Directions:

Write different math equations on the index cards. On the bottom, write three possible answers and punch a hole under each numeral as shown. On the back side, draw a circle around the correct response. The child takes an index card and a golf tee. The child inserts the golf tee into the hole next to the answer she chooses. She can then turn the card over to check her answer. Store the cards and golf tees in a zipper bag.

Variations:

Make similar games for alphabetical order, numerical order, sets and numerals, sight words, or initial consonant sounds. Older children can use this game format for a question and answer review.

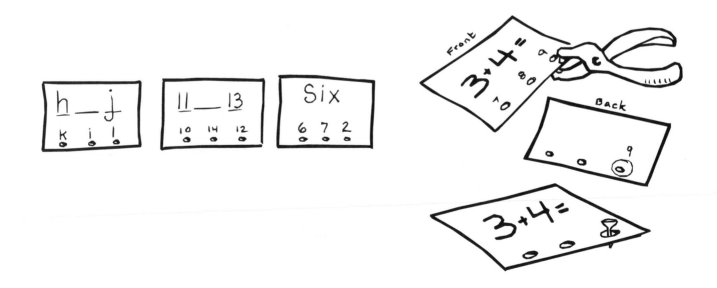

Bean Counters

The bean counter is an effective way to introduce measurement to children.

Materials:

- large lima beans
- clear packaging tape

Directions:

Lay out a piece of packaging tape (approximately 10" long), sticky side up on the table. Place ten beans side by side in the middle of the tape as shown. Fold both sides of the tape over the beans. Seal the ends and trim. Let the children use the bean counter to measure "how many beans long" various objects are. Challenge the children to find something three beans long or seven beans long. Ask them what they could do if they wanted to measure something longer than their bean counter.

Variations:

Use bean counters to practice counting by tens or to introduce place value.

Make similar counters out of pasta, Styrofoam peanuts, and other flat objects.

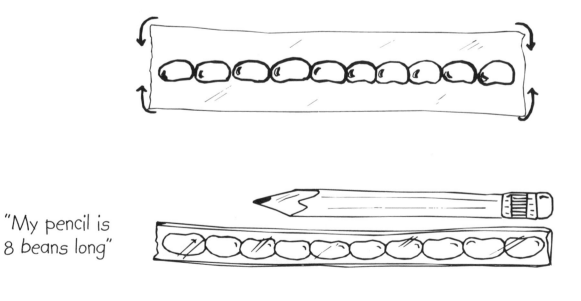

"My pencil is 8 beans long"

Pick-Up

Here's a team game where children will need to focus and listen so they can help score for their side.

Materials:

- poster board or heavy paper cut in 6" squares (26 pieces)
- markers

Directions:

Write a different letter on each piece of poster board. Divide the children into two teams and have them stand in lines about ten feet apart, facing each other. Scatter the cards face up on the floor between the two lines. Select one child from each team. Call out one of the letters; the first child to find that letter on the floor and pick it up may keep it for his team. The team with the most letters at the end of the game wins.

Variations:

Print sight words, numerals, shapes, or other information you want to reinforce on the cards.

Tangrams

Tangrams contribute to an understanding of mathematical concepts as well as problem-solving and motor skills.

Materials:

- tangram patterns (see following page)
- felt or heavy cardboard
- scissors
- zipper bag
- index cards

Directions:

Cut tangram shapes out of felt or heavy cardboard using the patterns on the following page. Draw tangram patterns on index cards for the children to reproduce. Encourage the children to explore with the shapes and create their own objects, then put out the patterns for them to copy.

Variations:

Increase the complexity of the patterns as the children become more proficient.

Rabbit

Snake

Bird

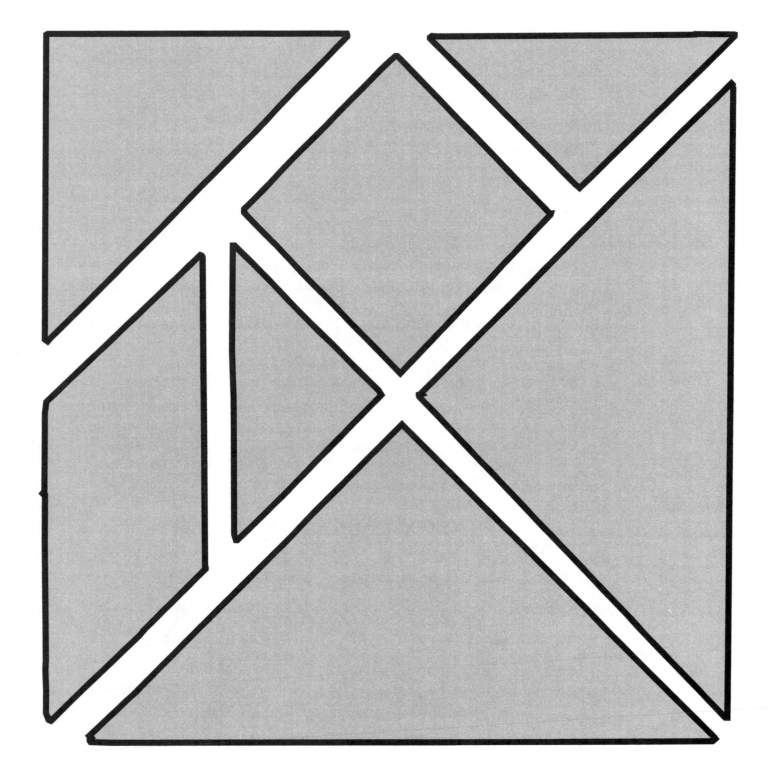

Snake Eyes

Children will be counting and recognizing numerals as they play this game of chance.

Materials:

- 2 dice
- score card for each child
- pen or pencil

Directions:

Give each child a score card and a pen or pencil. One at a time children take turns rolling the dice. They can count the number of dots on each die, then mark off the resulting numeral on their score cards. The first child to scratch off all of his two's (1 + 1 = snake eyes) wins!

Variations:

For older children, write numerals from 2 to 12, then let them add up their dice to mark off numerals on their score card.

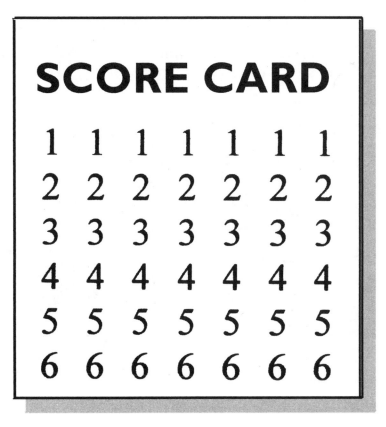

Eggs in a Nest

Counting, numeral recognition, sorting, and joining sets can become meaningful with this game.

Materials:

- paper lunch sacks
- colored pom poms
- small squares of paper
- marker

Directions:

Open the lunch sacks and roll them down as you mold them into nests. Print numerals on the squares of paper and place one in each nest. Have the children count out the appropriate number of eggs (pom poms) and place them in each nest.

Variations:

Ask the children to sort the pom poms by color into nests.

Write number words on the nests for the children to read and make sets.

Let children join and separate sets with the eggs in the nests.

You can also use cotton balls for eggs, or have the children mold their own eggs out of clay or play dough.